Terms and conditions

IMPORTANT – PERMITTED USE AND WARNINGS – READ CAREFULLY BEFORE USING

IF YOU ACCEPT THE ABOVE CONDITIONS YOU MAY PROCEED TO USE THE CD-ROM.

Recommended system requirements:

- Windows: XP (Service Pack 3), Vista (Service Pack 2) or Windows 7 with 2.33GHz processor
- Mac: OS 10.6 to 10.8 with Intel Core™ Duo processor
- 1GB RAM (recommended)
- 1024 x 768 Screen resolution
- CD-ROM drive (24x speed recommended)
- 16-bit sound card
- Microsoft Word

For all technical support queries, please phone Scholastic Customer Services on 0845 6039091.

SCHOLASTIC

Book End, Range Road, Witney, Oxfordshire, OX29 0YD

www.scholastic.co.uk

© 2014, Scholastic Ltd

1 2 3 4 5 6 7 8 9   4 5 6 7 8 9 0 1 2 3

British Library Cataloguing-in-Publication Data
A catalogue record for this book is available from the
British Library.

ISBN 978-1407-14084-1
Printed by Bell & Bain Ltd, Glasgow

Author
David Ashworth

Editorial Team
Robin Hunt, Harriet Power

Cover Design
Nicolle Thomas

Design Team
Nicolle Thomas and Andrea Lewis

Contents

Introduction

The aspiration of the National Curriculum for Music at Key Stages 1 and 2 is to provide a *high-quality music education which should engage and inspire pupils to develop a love of music and their talent as musicians, and so increase their self-confidence, creativity and sense of achievement.* Music lessons in primary schools should predominantly be active, practical experiences rather than a mere transmission of facts about music and its history. Children should learn about music through making music themselves, rather than simply learning about how others have made music in the past. This approach is reflected throughout the activities in this book.

100 Music Lessons: Planning Guide takes the subject content of the National Curriculum and uses it to provide weekly lesson ideas for Years 1 to 6. These ideas are grouped into six half-termly segments. They are structured to cover all areas of the National Curriculum subject content with suitable progression for each year, and can be used as a springboard for devising exciting Schemes of Work across Key Stages 1 and 2.

The lesson ideas should be used flexibly to suit your teaching and the children's learning. Establish your priorities and adapt them to the needs of the children in your school. For example, if singing is identified as an area for improvement in your school, make sure that you allocate more time for it than other activities. You may wish to swap the order of some of the lessons, and expand on certain activities while dedicating less time to others. The last week of each half term is a 'review' week that can be used as a breathing space to consolidate the children's learning, and to review any activities that children struggled with during the half term or did not have time to complete.

Music teaching in primary schools should be for all children and all teachers. Most of the activities in this book can be delivered by the non-specialist classroom teacher; those who are less confident in teaching music can use the 'Background knowledge' sections to help navigate some of the trickier lesson ideas. However, some of the activities may require a bit more specialist knowledge (such as those that use staff notation), and it is unfortunately beyond the scope of this book to go into detail about music theory. Non-specialists may therefore require some support to get the most out of the lesson ideas in this book, although classroom teachers should always remember that they are best placed to understand the needs of their children, and to make day-to-day links between music and work in other curriculum areas.

Terminology

In these medium-term plans, the main terms used are:

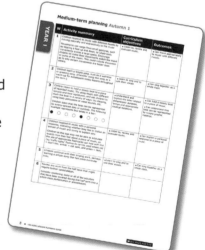

- **Activity summary:** a brief summary of the main activity for each lesson. This can be used to devise a more detailed lesson plan.
- **Curriculum objectives:** these are taken directly from the 'aims' of the National Curriculum for Music. They can be used to gain a quick idea of the main focus of a lesson.
- **Outcomes:** these are the skills and knowledge that children should be able to demonstrate at the end of the lesson or unit of work.

Some of the activities refer to musical terminology that may be unfamiliar to a non-specialist. While we have tried to explain as many of the terms as possible (whether in the activity summaries themselves or in the 'Background knowledge' sections at the end of each year), non-specialists may need to seek help to understand some of the more complex musical concepts that are introduced.

Assessment

■SCHOLASTIC

Teachers should provide continuous formative assessment that gently, but firmly, encourages and steers children towards becoming better at making music. Summative assessment can also be carried out at the end of activities that result in a performance or composition. Many of the activities in this book encourage peer assessment, where children evaluate each other's performances or compositions in order to improve their critical listening skills as well as their own work. Video or audio recordings can be very useful for assessment purposes, and teachers should get into the habit of recording children's practical work in this manner whenever possible.

About the book

The book provides content for each year group (Years 1–6) and includes:

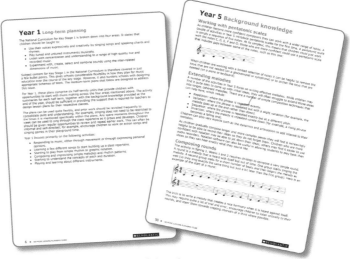

- **Long-term planning:** an overview of the learning outcomes and musical skills covered by each half-term unit.
- **Overview of progression:** a year-by-year overview of how children progress in their musical skills and understanding, based on the areas covered in the National Curriculum subject content.
- **Medium-term planning:** six half-termly grids for each year group. Each grid contains an overview of each week's planning, the outcomes for that week and the objectives covered.
- **Background knowledge:** an explanation of the key concepts and musical knowledge introduced in each year, to help support teachers' knowledge.

About the CD-ROM

The CD-ROM provides the Long-term planning, Overview of progression, Medium-term planning and Background knowledge as editable Word files. These can be used and adapted to meet the needs of your school. There is a simple menu screen on the CD-ROM; simply navigate to the year group you require and then click on the button to open the associated file. You will also find some additional resources, including 12 sample music lessons, at **www.scholastic.co.uk/100music**.

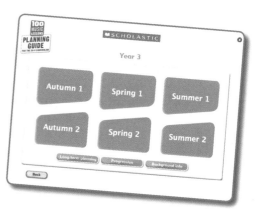

About the poster

The poster summarises the progression of key concepts in the National Curriculum for music. Display it in a central location, such as the staffroom, to help improve understanding of the new curriculum within your school.

Year 1 Long-term planning

The National Curriculum for Key Stage 1 is broken down into four areas. It states that children should be taught to:

- Use their voices expressively and creatively by singing songs and speaking chants and rhymes.
- Play tuned and untuned instruments musically.
- Listen with concentration and understanding to a range of high-quality live and recorded music.
- Experiment with, create, select and combine sounds using the inter-related dimensions of music.

Subject content for Key Stage 1 in the National Curriculum is therefore covered in just a few bullet points. This gives schools considerable flexibility in how they plan for music education over the course of the key stage. However, it also burdens schools with designing appropriate Schemes of Work. The medium-term plans that follow are designed to address this issue.

For Year 1, these plans comprise six half-termly units that provide children with opportunities to start with music making across the four areas mentioned above. The activity summaries for each half term, together with the background knowledge provided at the end of the year, should be sufficient in providing the support that is required for teachers to design lesson plans for their respective classes.

The plans can be used quite flexibly, and prior work should be revisited frequently to consolidate skills and understanding. For example, singing does not need to be restricted to the times it is mentioned specifically within the plans. Any spare moments throughout the week can be used to sing through the class repertoire as it grows and develops. Children should be given regular opportunities to review and repeat earlier work. This can often be informal and self-directed; for example, encourage children to work on action songs and singing games in their playground time.

Year 1 focuses primarily on the following activities:

- Responding to music, either through movement or through expressing personal opinions.
- Learning a few different songs to start building up a class repertoire.
- Starting to play from simple rhythm or graphic notation.
- Composing and improvising simple melodies and rhythm patterns.
- Starting to understand the concepts of pitch and duration.
- Playing and learning about different instruments.

Overview of progression in Year 1

One of the biggest challenges for the primary teacher is to find opportunities for all of the children in a class to build upon the musical experiences they have already had. These experiences will vary widely across the class, sometimes making differentiation a difficult feat. However, the early activities in Year 1 can be used to build some initial impressions of the musical capabilities of a class. These early indicators will not necessarily provide reliable pointers regarding musical potential for the future, but they can help the teacher to pitch and differentiate activities at an appropriate level, making sure that everyone in the class is given the opportunity to progress.

Based on the subject content for Key Stage 1 (outlined on the previous page), progression in Year 1 can be summarised as follows:

Using voices expressively and creatively

Over the course of Year 1, children will build up their repertoire by learning a number of new songs. To begin with, children will sing together as a whole class. In the second half term it is suggested that the class is split into smaller groups, which alternate different sections of a song. Towards the end of the year, children can start to add actions to their songs; this exercise in multitasking is a great precursor to combining singing with an instrumental accompaniment.

Playing tuned and untuned instruments musically

During Year 1 children are given a number of opportunities to play instruments in different contexts. They are encouraged to play with a steady pulse, using very basic notation as a guide. They learn to play rhythms that incorporate beats and rests, and to play very simple melodies. Children also learn to play music as part of a group, where they have to listen to each other and take turns to contribute at the appropriate point.

Listening with concentration and understanding

Throughout the course of the year, children are asked to listen and respond to recorded extracts of music. These responses are initially through movement, which may be free and expressive or more directed and controlled. As children progress, their movements should more accurately reflect the pulse and character of the music.

Children are also asked to voice their personal opinions about a piece of music, learning appropriate ways to describe and talk about music.

Creating, selecting and combining sounds

During Year 1 children are provided with opportunities to select and combine sounds in various ways. To start with children might work with short, individual sounds; over the course of the year there are opportunities to combine sounds together to create more musical phrases (such as short melodies or rhythm patterns). As children become more confident, they should aim to select sounds that are appropriate for the context and use them musically.

Medium-term planning Autumn 1

YEAR 1

W	Activity summary	Curriculum objectives	Outcomes
1	Children respond to music with different moods by moving naturally and expressively to the music. Movements can range from small gestures, such as tapping a foot up and down, to whole body movements across a large space. Encourage children to make their movements match the mood or pulse of the music. This could include discussion as to why certain movements are better than others.	• Listen to, review and evaluate music.	• Can move appropriately to music with different moods.
2	Children learn a simple song, such as a welcome or greeting song. (Consider using this song as a warm-up for subsequent music lessons throughout the term.)	• Learn to sing and to use their voices.	• Can sing together as a whole class.
3	Children learn to hold a steady beat to a piece of recorded music. Try using music with different tempos and time signatures, and ask children to mark the beat in a variety of ways: by clapping, using body percussion or vocal sounds, and so on. Children learn that the beat can be represented by evenly-spaced dots or symbols. The following example represents four beats in a bar: ● ○ ○ ○ ● ○ ○ ○	• Understand and explore the inter-related dimensions: duration, tempo and appropriate musical notations.	• Can hold a steady beat to a piece of music. • Can understand that beat can be represented by simple graphic notation.
4	Children respond to music with a personal response, indicating whether they like or dislike an extract of music and trying to explain why. Children at this age may not be able to articulate exactly how they feel about a piece of music, so the use of appropriate flashcards can help with this (such as 'traffic lights' flashcards can be used where red = don't like, amber = not sure, and green = like).	• Listen to, review and evaluate music.	• Can explain a personal response to a piece of music.
5	Children continue with their singing work, perhaps learning a simple song that has cross-curricular links.	• Learn to sing and to use their voices.	• Can sing together as a whole class.
6	Review any work from the half term that might require further consolidation. Consider combining some or all of the activities that have been covered during this half term into a whole-class performance or presentation.		

Medium-term planning Autumn 2

W	Activity summary	Curriculum objectives	Outcomes
1	Children review the songs learned in Autumn 1 and add a further simple song to their repertoire. The class splits into two groups and each group sings alternate sections of a song.	• Learn to sing and to use their voices.	• Can take turns singing different sections of a song.
2	Children develop a sense of relative pitch by responding to high and low sounds through movement. Sing or play a series of notes that include high and low pitches. Children respond to the changes in pitch through movement (for example, by standing up for a high note or crouching for a low note). Then reverse the roles: the teacher indicates high or low by moving their hand up or down in the air. Children follow the changes in pitch with their voices (for example, by gliding from a low note to a high note as your hand rises).	• Understand and explore the inter-related dimensions (pitch).	• Can differentiate with increasing accuracy between high and low pitch.
3	Children find sounds to represent the characters, events or moods in a story or poem. Children can explore different ways of singing or playing classroom instruments to find the sounds that best match the characters, events or moods that they are trying to portray (such as a loud rattle for an angry character or quiet tapping to represent falling rain).	• Have the opportunity to learn a musical instrument. • Create and compose music.	• Can choose appropriate sounds to represent different characters, events or moods.
4	Children continue their work from the previous week. They practise adding their sounds to a narration of the story or poem.	• Create and compose music. • Perform music.	• Can play appropriate sounds at specific points during a narration.
5	Children develop their knowledge of different instruments by matching pictures of the instruments to recordings of them being played. There are various websites that can be used to support this activity, including the 'Instrument Match-Up' game on the BBC website (found in the 'Musical Mysteries' section on www.bbc.co.uk/schools). Children could take turns to come to the front of the class and drag the instruments into the correct boxes.	• Listen to, review and evaluate music. • Understand and explore the inter-related dimensions (timbre).	• Can identify certain instruments, if not by name then by family (such as brass, woodwind, strings or percussion).
6	Review any work from the half term that might require further consolidation. Consider combining some or all of the activities that have been covered during this half term into a whole-class performance or presentation.		

Notes:
Visit the Scholastic website (www.scholastic.co.uk/100music) to find a sample lesson covering week 3's work on finding sounds to represent characters, events or moods in a story or poem.

Medium-term planning Spring 1

W	Activity summary	Curriculum objectives	Outcomes
1	In two groups, children respond through movement to music with contrasting moods. Each group takes turns to observe and evaluate the other one. Children then select appropriate words from a set of flashcards to describe an extract of music. Cards should refer to aspects of the music such as the instruments, inter-related dimensions, character and mood.	• Listen to, review and evaluate music. • Understand and explore the inter-related dimensions.	• Can respond to the character of music through movement. • Can identify certain musical features by ear.
2	Children sing a well-known song in a variety of ways (for example, spoken, whispered, quietly, loudly, smoothly, slowly and quickly). This activity can be used to explore concepts such as tempo, dynamics and articulation.	• Learn to sing and to use their voices.	• Can sing expressively. • Can recognise that the same piece of music can be performed in different ways.
3	Similar to Year 1, Autumn 1, Week 3, children hold a steady beat to extracts of music with different tempos and time signatures. They learn to emphasis the first beat of the bar (for example, by clapping louder on this beat). With guidance, children work out how many beats there are to a bar in each extract. They notate the number of beats using the graphic notation mentioned in Year 1, Autumn 1, Week 3.	• Understand and explore the inter-related dimensions: duration and appropriate musical notations.	• Can hold a steady beat to a piece of music. • Can use simple graphic notation to notate the number of beats in a bar.
4	Children improvise short melodies by ear using just a few notes. Encourage children to use different rhythms (such as long and short notes) as they improvise. Find a way to record the melodies for use in next week's lesson (for example, with an MP3 recorder or computer-based software such as *Audacity*).	• Create and compose music. • Understand and explore the inter-related dimensions: pitch and duration.	• Can improvise melodies using different pitches and rhythms.
5	Children continue to develop their melodies from the previous week, refining and extending them into longer compositions. Some children perform their work to the rest of the class.	• Create and compose music. • Perform music.	• Can develop and extend melodies to create a longer composition.
6	Review any work from the half term that might require further consolidation. Consider combining some or all of the activities that have been covered during this half term into a whole-class performance or presentation.		

Medium-term planning Spring 2

W	Activity summary	Curriculum objectives	Outcomes
1	Using MP3 recorders or similar equipment, children record natural and man-made sounds in their local environment (possibly as part of a nature/town walk). In the classroom they play back, identify and describe the sounds, developing their understanding of musical terminology.	• Use technology appropriately. • Listen to, review and evaluate music.	• Can listen to environmental sounds and make choices regarding which ones are worth recording. • Can use simple recording equipment.
2	Children find ways to represent the sounds collected in week 1 through music, by using body percussion, vocal sounds or instruments. Encourage children to replicate the sounds as closely as possible. These sounds could be put together into a short piece or soundscape to be performed by the whole class.	• Create and compose music. • Perform music.	• Can select and use sounds appropriately to create a specific musical effect.
3	Children sit in a circle. Each child has an instrument which they play in turn: when one child stops playing, the next one starts, until everyone in the circle has played a short phrase. Shout 'switch!' to change the direction of the circle. Next, the circle only has one instrument. One child plays it while making eye contact with another child, who gets up and takes the instrument from them, continuing to play as they go back to their place. This process is repeated. As the children's concentration develops, introduce more instruments into the circle.	• Have the opportunity to learn a musical instrument. • Create and compose music.	• Can improvise simple rhythms and tunes. • Can perform as part of a group.
4	Children review any of the songs learned so far this year. Certain sections of the songs are sung by small groups or soloists.	• Learn to sing and to use their voices.	• Can sing solo or in a small group. • Can take turns singing different sections of a song.
5	Children read from a series of pictures (objects, animals, shapes etc) ordered from left to right on a whiteboard. Each child (or small group of children) has a sound represented by a corresponding picture within the sequence, which they play as the teacher points to the pictures in turn. Try arranging the symbols in different ways, and engage the class in discussion as to which sequences they think work best.	• Understand and explore how music is created using appropriate musical notations.	• Can play simple pieces from symbols (pictures), reading from left to right. • Can follow a conductor and understand when to play by listening to others.
6	Review any work from the half term that might require further consolidation. Consider combining some or all of the activities that have been covered during this half term into a whole-class performance or presentation.		

Notes:
Visit the Scholastic website (www.scholastic.co.uk/100music) to find a sample lesson covering week 1's work on the recording of natural and man-made sounds in the local environment.

Medium-term planning Summer 1

YEAR 1

W	Activity summary	Curriculum objectives	Outcomes
1	Children review any of the songs learned so far this year, and add another simple song to their repertoire. Start the singing session with some vocal warm-ups to help prepare the children for better-quality singing. Many suitable warm-ups can be found by searching online for 'vocal warm-ups for kids'.	• Learn to sing and to use their voices.	• Can use vocal warm-ups as a preparation for singing.
2	Perform a repeated action, using body percussion or vocal sounds, in time to a piece of music (for example, taps their knees on the beat). Children copy the action. Once established, change to a new action. Gradually combine different actions in more complex ways (for example, alternating claps and clicks in a simple rhythm).	• Understand and explore the inter-related dimensions: duration. • Perform music.	• Can respond accurately to the pulse in music. • Can copy simple rhythm patterns.
3	Children listen to extracts of music with contrasting moods. They discuss and rehearse appropriate movements for the music, subsequently adding their movements to the music as they listen again. Instead of moving spontaneously to music in a free and improvised way, children imagine and plan the movements in advance. They need to find ways of describing or demonstrating those movements to others in their group. The second part of the task involves memorising and recalling the movements as the music is replayed.	• Listen to, review and evaluate music.	• Can respond to music through movement in more structured ways.
4	Children perform simple ostinato patterns to accompany a well-known vocal rhyme or chant. The teacher takes a short section of the rhyme or chant (for example, a few words) and asks children to repeat it in a loop. Children then transfer this repeated rhythm to percussion instruments. The ostinato acts as an accompaniment to the whole rhyme. Try repeating this process with different rhymes and chants, or different rhythms. This activity can be used to explore the concept of texture (there are two parts to the texture here: the accompaniment and the chant).	• Understand and explore the inter-related dimensions: duration and texture. • Have the opportunity to learn a musical instrument.	• Can perform a rhythmic ostinato pattern.
5	Split the class into different groups, and ask each group to practise one of the rhythm patterns learned in the previous week. Order these patterns into a structure to create a whole piece, where each group has to perform their pattern at the correct time.	• Have the opportunity to learn a musical instrument. • Perform music.	• Can perform repeated patterns in a defined structure.
6	Review any work from the half term that might require further consolidation. Consider combining some or all of the activities that have been covered during this half term into a whole-class performance or presentation.		

Medium-term planning Summer 2

W	Activity summary	Curriculum objectives	Outcomes
1	Children develop a sense of rhythm by performing simple actions to accompany their singing (for example, by learning an action song). This builds on previous work by combining two areas of activity: movement and singing. This multi-tasking is a valuable skills-building exercise that can be used as a precursor to combining singing with an instrumental accompaniment.	• Learn to sing and to use their voices.	• Can sing with a sense of rhythm. • Can combine singing with appropriate actions.
2	Similar to Year 1, Spring 2, Week 5, a score is created from pictures of percussion instruments ordered into a sequence. Each group of children plays their percussion instrument at the right point in the sequence. This activity involves making decisions about the order of the sequence. Children also need to work out what they are going to play on their designated instrument. This could be improvised or worked out in advance. The ultimate aim is to make sure that the sequence of sounds develops in a musically satisfying way.	• Understand and explore how music is created using appropriate musical notations. • Create and compose music.	• Can organise symbols and sounds into musical structures.
3	Repeat the previous week's activity, but now give children the opportunity to work in smaller or different groups, with different instruments and pictures.	• Understand and explore how music is created using appropriate musical notations. • Create and compose music.	• Can organise symbols and sounds into musical structures.
4	Children compose or improvise sounds in response to a picture journey or trail (for example, a journey around town or the life cycle of a frog). Children will have to create appropriate sounds or musical phrases for each stage in the journey. This could involve discussion as to which sounds are the most effective, and why.	• Create and compose music.	• Can choose appropriate sounds to represent different pictures or situations.
5	Children continue their work from the previous week. They develop and refine their sounds, structuring them into a complete piece to be performed by the whole class.	• Create and compose music. • Perform music.	• Can play sounds at the appropriate times in a structured performance.
6	Review any work from the half term that might require further consolidation. Consider combining some or all of the activities that have been covered during this half term into a whole-class performance or presentation.		

Year 1 Background knowledge

Singing

Singing should be an inclusive activity with an emphasis on enjoyment, building confidence and developing relationships. As the year progresses, find opportunities to give all children the chance to sing in small groups or solo if they wish. Once warm-ups are introduced, aim to use these regularly: they could be used to warm up children before any type of activity, whether it involves singing or not. Find opportunities for 'little but often' singing, such as singing the register or singing in breaks between other curriculum activities.

Playing instruments

In addition to encouraging 'correct' playing of instruments, using standard techniques, let children explore more unconventional ways of playing instruments to produce a fuller range of sounds. Encourage safe, responsible playing so that any potential damage is avoided (either to the instruments or the children playing them). Establish ground rules for when to start and stop playing.

Composing and improvising

Composition is a grand term for what is essentially a very natural activity for young children. Children are fascinated by different sounds and will want to make up patterns using those sounds. In the context of the primary music classroom, this is composition. Teachers can help to facilitate this activity by organising the class into small groups for collaborative composition, providing suitable frameworks or stimuli, and ensuring appropriate sound sources are made readily available.

Improvisation is essentially a more spontaneous, less structured type of composition. It involves making up music and playing it on the spot, rather than thinking more carefully about how to organise and structure the sounds. In Year 1, the distinction between the two terms is largely irrelevant; as children progress, their compositions should start to sound less like improvisations (ie more carefully planned and structured rather than made up on the spot).

Producing graphic resources

Some of the activities in this year use graphic notation: notation consisting of symbols and pictures. Consider producing this on a computer so it can be projected on to a screen that all children can see. Presentation software, such as PowerPoint, has a good range of design features that can be used to produce graphic scores, and a sequence of slides can be used for more extended work. Switching off the lights usually makes the screen more visible and can create a more suitable atmosphere for a musical performance, where there is less visual distraction for performers and listeners.

Understanding beat

A couple of the activities in this year introduce the concept of beat. This is simply a constant pulse that underpins the music: if you can clap along at a steady pace to a piece of music, you are probably clapping the beat. While there is not enough room here to go into detail about beat and how it is notated, there are two related concepts that are worth learning about:

- **Bars:** staff notation divides beats into chunks called bars. In a piece of music every bar will have the same number of beats. The bars are divided by vertical lines (barlines).
- **Time signatures:** the time signature at the start of a piece of notation will tell you how many beats there are to each bar. Four beats to a bar is most common (and indicated by the time signature $\frac{4}{4}$).

Year 2 Long-term planning

Year 2 is based on the same subject content as Year 1, which states that children should be taught to:

- Use their voices expressively and creatively by singing songs and speaking chants and rhymes.
- Play tuned and untuned instruments musically.
- Listen with concentration and understanding to a range of high-quality live and recorded music.
- Experiment with, create, select and combine sounds using the inter-related dimensions of music.

The medium-term plans that follow comprise six half-termly units that provide children with opportunities to progress with music making across the four areas mentioned above. The activity summaries for each half term, together with the background knowledge provided at the end of the year, should be sufficient in providing the support that is required for teachers to design lesson plans for their respective classes.

As with Year 1, teachers will want to use these plans flexibly and adapt them to their requirements. They will want to think about prioritising certain activities, while at the same time maintaining a broad and balanced curriculum. For example, if singing has been perceived as a weakness across the school then more time could be given to this activity. If cross-curricular work is deemed important then opportunities can easily be found to make links to other subjects. At the same time, schools will want to play to their strengths. If the school is fortunate enough to have access to instrumental teachers, for example, then their expertise should be called upon wherever possible.

Year 2 focuses primarily on the following activities:

- Responding to and evaluating music, including the children's own compositions.
- Learning slightly more complicated songs.
- Playing from and notating rhythm grids.
- Carrying out various composition activities.
- Exploring the inter-related dimensions (in particular pitch, duration and structure).
- Playing and learning about different instruments.

Overview of progression in Year 2

In Year 2 children will consolidate and build on the skills and understanding covered during the previous year. Some of the activities use similar starting points to those provided in Year 1, but with the aim of taking the learning further and deeper.

Based on the subject content for Key Stage 1 (outlined on the previous page), progression in Year 2 can be summarised as follows:

Using voices expressively and creatively

During Year 2 children are given opportunities to review old songs as well as to learn new ones. While children will primarily sing together as a whole class, they should also be given opportunities to sing in small groups or on their own – something they should become more comfortable with as their confidence grows. Children are also encouraged to sing more expressively, paying attention to aspects such as dynamics and articulation.

In Spring 2 children are asked to 'drop out' in certain passages of a song, singing the words silently in their heads. This allows children to make a conscious start in developing audiation, which is an important skill for any musician.

Playing tuned and untuned instruments musically

During Year 2 children are given a number of opportunities to play instruments in different contexts. Quite a few of the activities involve playing from notation, requiring greater accuracy and control over pitch and rhythm. Children are also given more opportunities to rehearse and evaluate their own playing, allowing them to become familiar with the idea that practising is an important part of becoming a more competent musician.

Children continue to learn to play music as part of a group, where they have to listen to each other and take turns to contribute at the appropriate points.

Listening with concentration and understanding

In Year 2 children continue to listen to recorded extracts of music, and are now given the opportunity to respond through painting and drawing.

Children are also expected to listen to and evaluate their own compositions. This requires children to listen carefully, identify the features that work well or need improvement, and articulate why. Children are likely to find this challenging to start with and may need a lot of support, but they should gradually learn what features to listen out for and how to talk about them.

Creating, selecting and combining sounds

During Year 2 children will think more carefully about how to select and structure sounds appropriately. They will work with beginnings, middles and endings in their compositions. They will also spend more time evaluating their own compositions, using these critiques to learn how to improve their work in the future.

Medium-term planning Autumn 1

W	Activity summary	Curriculum objectives	Outcomes
1	Children review some of the songs learned in Year 1. Different sections of the songs are sung by different children, so they get used to singing in smaller groups. Children plan an imaginary concert consisting of the songs learned in Year 1. They should order the songs into an effective sequence.	• Learn to sing and to use their voices. • Listen to, review and evaluate music.	• Can recall songs learned during the previous year. • Can think about how to order a concert effectively.
2	Children play from simple rhythm grids that incorporate silent beats, while maintaining a steady pulse. Children compose their own rhythm patterns, incorporating silent beats, and notate these using rhythm grids.	• Understand and explore how music is created using appropriate musical notations. • Create and compose music.	• Can perform with a steady pulse and a correct number of beats and rests. • Can compose and notate simple rhythm patterns.
3	Children swap their rhythm grids from the previous week and perform each other's patterns. Children explore playing the patterns on different instruments. In small groups, children order their patterns into an effective sequence to create a short piece. They rehearse this piece and perform it to the rest of the class.	• Understand and explore how music is created using appropriate musical notations. • Create and compose music.	• Can perform with a steady pulse and a correct number of beats and rests.
4	Children listen to and describe a piece of music. They talk about how the music makes them feel and then draw or paint a picture that they think is representative of the piece. Children should share and evaluate their pictures: which best capture the mood of the music, and why? Links can be made in this activity to artists who have a strong connection to music (for example, Kandinsky and Klee).	• Listen to, review and evaluate music.	• Can draw a picture that is representative of a piece of music. • Can share and evaluate work.
5	Children sing a song they have already learned and try to dissect its structure. Which bits are repeated? Which bits are different? Find a way to represent the structure pictorially (for example, using different colours for different sections). Children listen to another song from a contrasting genre and identify the repeated sections within the song (for example, a repeated line or chorus).	• Learn to sing and to use their voices. • Understand and explore the inter-related dimensions: structure. • Listen to, review and evaluate music.	• Can identify different sections within a song.
6	Review any work from the half term that might require further consolidation. Consider combining some or all of the activities that have been covered during this half term into a whole-class performance or presentation.		

Notes:
Visit the Scholastic website (www.scholastic.co.uk/100music) to find a sample lesson covering week 2's work on playing music using simple rhythm grids.

Medium-term planning Autumn 2

W	Activity summary	Curriculum objectives	Outcomes
1	Children compose sounds and musical phrases to represent characters, moods or events in a story or poem. This is similar to the activity in Year 1, Autumn 2, Week 3, but students should now demonstrate a little more sophistication and variety in their choice of sounds.	• Have the opportunity to learn a musical instrument. • Create and compose music.	• Can choose appropriate sounds to represent different characters, events or moods.
2	Children continue their work from the previous week, structuring their sounds into a complete piece. Children should refine their pieces through rehearsal, performance and evaluation.	• Create and compose music. • Perform music. • Listen to, review and evaluate music.	• Can perform with accuracy and control. • Can improve their work through rehearsal and evaluation.
3	Children respond to short pitch patterns through movement (for example, low-high = step forward; high-low = step back; high-high = jump on the spot). Children then use vocal sounds, or suitable instruments (for example, xylophones), to play simple phrases from notation that indicates different pitches (for example, three different notes: low, middle and high).	• Understand and explore the inter-related dimensions: pitch. • Understand and explore how music is created using appropriate musical notations.	• Can recognise and respond to differences in pitch. • Can perform from simple pitch notation.
4	Children discuss effective ways to structure a piece. In groups, they decide on an overall structure for a piece they are going to compose (for example, a beginning with a bright, happy idea; a contrasting middle; an ending that repeats the opening idea but louder to create a climax). Children start to compose their own pieces using the structures they have chosen.	• Understand and explore the inter-related dimensions: structure. • Create and compose music.	• Can understand how to structure a piece of music. • Can compose music to a given structure.
5	Children develop and rehearse their compositions from the previous week, before performing them to the rest of the class.	• Create and compose music. • Perform music.	• Can compose music to a given structure. • Can perform with accuracy and control.
6	Review any work from the half term that might require further consolidation. Consider combining some or all of the activities that have been covered during this half term into a whole-class performance or presentation.		

Medium-term planning Spring 1

W	Activity summary	Curriculum objectives	Outcomes
1	Children continue working with rhythm grids (see Year 2, Autumn 2, Week 3). Children play from rhythm grids that indicate beats and rests. They then compose their own rhythm patterns and notate them using grids. Building on the work done in Autumn 2, children should now aim to introduce more variety into their patterns, making good use of both beats and rests.	• Understand and explore how music is created using appropriate musical notations. • Create and compose music.	• Can compose and perform from rhythm grids that indicate beats and rests.
2	Children swap their rhythm grids from the previous week and perform each other's patterns. Children explore playing the patterns on different instruments. In small groups, children order their patterns into an effective sequence to create a short piece. They rehearse and perform the piece to the rest of the class.	• Create and compose music. • Perform music.	• Can perform with a steady pulse and a correct number of beats and rests.
3	Children listen to extracts of music that are performed by different voices (for example, men, women and children). They learn to identify who is singing, and find ways to describe how they can tell. Next, children try to identify an instrument playing a solo part in a recorded piece (for example, a guitar solo in a pop song or a piano solo in a concerto). Children have a selection of pictures and names to choose from.	• Listen to, review and evaluate music.	• Can identify different types of voice in a song. • Can identify certain instruments, if not by name then by family (such as brass, woodwind, strings or percussion).
4	Children learn a song that includes silent passages (such as 'Heads, Shoulders, Knees and Toes' where children omit a body part on each repetition of the song). This activity helps to develop an important musical ability: audiation. This means the process of mentally hearing music when the sound itself is not physically present.	• Learn to sing and to use their voices.	• Can remain quiet, but still keep a sense of pulse, in certain passages of a song.
5	Children rehearse and perform the song from the previous week (including the silent passages). The teacher records their performance (for example, using an MP3 recorder). Children then try to sing along to their own recording, maintaining a steady pulse. This activity can be used to explore the concept of tempo, as children will have to sing at the same tempo as their recording in order to stay in time with it.	• Learn to sing and to use their voices. • Understand and explore the inter-related dimensions: tempo.	• Can remain quiet, but still keep a sense of pulse, in certain passages of a song. • Can understand the concept of tempo.
6	Review any work from the half term that might require further consolidation. Consider combining some or all of the activities that have been covered during this half term into a whole-class performance or presentation.		

Medium-term planning Spring 2

W	Activity summary	Curriculum objectives	Outcomes
1	Children create group compositions, perhaps using ideas from the previous half term or a relevant cross-curricular topic (for example, a rainforest composition). Children rehearse, perform and record their compositions using suitable equipment (for example, an MP3 recorder or computer program such as *Audacity*).	• Create and compose music. • Use technology appropriately.	• Can contribute to a group composition. • Can use appropriate technology to record music.
2	Children listen to and evaluate their recordings from the previous week. They discuss how to improve their compositions and, if there is time, implement the necessary changes.	• Listen to, review and evaluate music.	• Can evaluate and improve their work.
3	Children sit in a circle, each with a percussion instrument. One child produces a sound. The next child plays the first sound and adds their own. The third child plays the first two sounds and adds another, and so on. Children develop the ability to recall patterns and reproduce sounds with increasing accuracy. This activity could be extended by using different rhythms and/or pitches to build up simple rhythm patterns and/or melodies.	• Have the opportunity to learn a musical instrument. • Create and compose music.	• Can remember and replicate patterns of increasing length and complexity.
4	Children perform from simple notation that uses different symbols to represent long and short notes (for example, a rectangle = long note, square = short note). The scores could also incorporate rests. Children could loop the rhythm patterns to provide an accompaniment for a recorded piece of music.	• Understand and explore how music is created using appropriate musical notations. • Understand and explore the inter-related dimensions: duration.	• Can perform from notation that indicates long and short rhythms.
5	Children review their work from the previous week. When this is secure, consider incorporating pitch into the notation as well (for example, high and low notes, which could be indicated by symbols that are placed higher or lower on the score).	• Understand and explore how music is created using appropriate musical notations. • Understand and explore the inter-related dimensions: duration and pitch.	• Can perform from notation that indicates rhythm and pitch.
6	Review any work from the half term that might require further consolidation. Consider combining some or all of the activities that have been covered during this half term into a whole-class performance or presentation.		

Notes:
Visit the Scholastic website (www.scholastic.co.uk/100music) to find a sample lesson covering week 4's work on performing from simple notation.

■SCHOLASTIC

Medium-term planning Summer 1

W	Activity summary	Curriculum objectives	Outcomes
1	In groups, children devise a mime and compose music to accompany it. For example, a mime about being on a rollercoaster could be accompanied by a swooping melody; a mime about a monster could be accompanied by scary, tense music. Children could consider using music technology to provide sound effects and/or an accompaniment, and combine this with vocal and/or instrumental sounds.	• Create and compose music. • Use technology appropriately.	• Can compose music to accompany a piece of drama.
2	Children finish and rehearse their compositions from the previous week. Each group performs its mime and the accompanying composition to the rest of the class.	• Create and compose music. • Perform music.	• Can perform music as an accompaniment to a piece of drama.
3	Children listen to an extract of music that evokes a particular mood. They discuss and rehearse appropriate movements for the music, subsequently adding their movements to the music as they listen again. Children then select appropriate words from a set of flashcards to describe the extract of music. Cards should refer to aspects of the music such as the instruments, inter-related dimensions, character and mood.	• Listen to, review and evaluate music. • Understand and explore the inter-related dimensions.	• Can respond to the character of music through movement. • Can identify certain musical features by ear.
4	Similar to Year 1, Summer 1, Week 4, children perform simple ostinato patterns to accompany a well-known vocal rhyme or chant. The teacher takes a short section of the rhyme or chant (for example, a few words), and asks children to repeat it in a loop. Children then transfer this repeated rhythm to instruments. The ostinato acts as an accompaniment to the whole rhyme. This activity could be extended by turning the ostinato rhythm into a simple melody (so it involves both rhythm and pitch).	• Understand and explore the inter-related dimensions: duration, pitch and texture. • Have the opportunity to learn a musical instrument.	• Can perform a rhythmic or melodic ostinato pattern.
5	Children review some of the songs they have learned so far, and perhaps add another one to their repertoire. Encourage children to sing more expressively. Consider singing different sections of a song with different dynamics (for example, quiet and loud) or articulation (for example, smooth and spiky).	• Learn to sing and to use their voices. • Understand and explore the inter-related dimensions: dynamics.	• Can sing expressively, with contrasting dynamics or articulation.
6	Review any work from the half term that might require further consolidation. Consider combining some or all of the activities that have been covered during this half term into a whole-class performance or presentation.		

Medium-term planning Summer 2

W	Activity summary	Curriculum objectives	Outcomes
1	Children find various sounds (vocal, body and percussion) to represent given symbols prepared by the teacher. Children order the symbols into simple sequences, from which they perform. This provides an opportunity to build on earlier work using notation, but with a wider range of sounds.	• Understand and explore how music is created using appropriate musical notations. • Create and compose music.	• Can perform from simple graphic notation and recognise that symbols can be used to represent sounds.
2	Children continue the previous week's work, varying the activity by using different sounds, symbols and instruments. This activity could be extended by using a two-part texture (ie two lines of symbols, one on top of the other, that are played simultaneously).	• Understand and explore how music is created using appropriate musical notations. • Create and compose music.	• Can perform from simple graphic notation and recognise that symbols can be used to represent sounds.
3	Children develop a sense of rhythm by performing actions to accompany their singing (for example, by learning an action song). This is similar to Year 1, Summer 2, Week 1, but could be made more challenging by assigning different portions of the song (or different actions) to different groups or soloists.	• Learn to sing and to use their voices.	• Can combine singing with appropriate actions. • Can sing solo or in a small group.
4	Similar to Year 1, Summer 2, Week 4, children compose or improvise sounds in response to a picture journey or trail. Children will have to create appropriate sounds or musical phrases for each stage in the journey. This could involve discussion as to which sounds are the most effective, and why.	• Create and compose music.	• Can choose appropriate sounds to represent different pictures or situations.
5	Children develop and refine the previous week's work, structuring the sounds into a complete piece that is then performed. Children evaluate each other's performances: how successful were they in representing the picture journey?	• Create and compose music. • Perform music.	• Can structure sounds appropriately to create a piece. • Can perform and evaluate a composition.
6	Review any work from the half term that might require further consolidation. Consider combining some or all of the activities that have been covered during this half term into a whole-class performance or presentation.		

Year 2 Background knowledge

Listening to music

The activity in Spring 1, Week 3 requires children to listen to a selection of vocal and instrumental recordings. This is a good opportunity to start building up a bank of recordings for your school. A number of teachers could contribute to this resource, gradually building it up over time so it covers a variety of styles and genres. The resulting bank of music is likely to prove useful for many activities, not just those focused on listening.

It is also worth building up a selection of useful websites, apps and computer programs that can be used to demonstrate different instruments or aspects of music.

Recording and assessing music

In Spring 2, Weeks 1 and 2 children are asked to record their own compositions and use the recordings for self and peer assessment. This is a routine that can be used at key points in the years that follow, providing opportunities for self, peer and teacher assessment. Teachers should get into the habit of audio or video recording their children's work whenever possible; the recordings can be invaluable for assessment purposes, but can also be used as models during class work, or to showcase children's achievements during assemblies and parents' evenings.

Smartphones, MP3 recorders, computers and video cameras can all be used to record children's work. From the start, devise a clear system for labelling and storing files so they are easy to retrieve.

Working with rhythm grids and simple graphic notation

A rhythm grid is essentially a table that contains dots indicating different rhythm patterns. It is read horizontally from left to right, and each box represents the same length of time (for example, one beat). For example, this grid represents a steady beat:

In this grid, the second and third notes should be played twice as fast as the first note:

Rests can also be added to the grid:

Spring 2, Weeks 4 and 5 introduce very simple graphic notation that can be used to indicate rhythm and pitch. An example might look like this:

This notation is read from left to right. Here the bottom row represents a low pitch and the top row a high pitch. A rectangle represents a long note while a square represents a short note. Blank boxes can be used to indicate rests.

Year 3 Long-term planning

The National Curriculum for Key Stage 2 is a little more detailed than for Key Stage 1, and is broken down into six areas. It states that children should be taught to:

- Play and perform in solo and ensemble contexts, using their voices and playing musical instruments with increasing accuracy, fluency, control and expression.
- Improvise and compose music for a range of purposes using the inter-related dimensions of music.
- Listen with attention to detail and recall sounds with increasing aural memory.
- Use and understand staff and other musical notations.
- Appreciate and understand a wide range of high-quality live and recorded music drawn from different traditions and from great composers and musicians.
- Develop an understanding of the history of music.

As for Key Stage 1, the main focus here is on performing, listening and composing or improvising. The two noticeable additions are the points regarding notation and the history of music. Graphic notation has already been covered in some of the Key Stage 1 activities; over the next few years children will gradually progress until they can read simple staff notation. An understanding of the history of music will be woven into various activities over the course of the key stage.

The medium-term plans that follow comprise six half-termly units that provide children with opportunities to progress with music making across the six areas mentioned above. The activity summaries for each half term, together with the background knowledge provided at the end of the year, should be sufficient in providing the support that is required for teachers to design lesson plans for their respective classes.

Year 3 focuses primarily on the following activities:

- Responding to and evaluating music, including the children's own compositions.
- Reviewing and building the class' repertoire of songs.
- Playing from and composing with notation, including one-line staves.
- Using technology to record and manipulate sounds.
- Cementing an understanding of the inter-related dimensions.
- Playing instruments in a variety of contexts.

Overview of progression in Year 3

In Year 3 children will consolidate and build on the skills and understanding covered during Key Stage 1. Some of the activities use similar starting points to those provided in Key Stage 1, but with the aim of taking the learning further and deeper.

Based on the subject content for Key Stage 2 (outlined on the previous page), progression in Year 3 can be summarised as follows:

Performing in solo and ensemble contexts

As with previous years, children are given various opportunities to perform both vocal and instrumental music. Children continue singing songs with silent passages (to improve their audiation), and learn a song with a call-and-response structure. The focus in this year is on singing and playing more expressively, for example by paying attention to dynamics and articulation.

Children also start to play pieces where there is more than one layer, requiring them to hold their own part against a contrasting one.

Improvising and composing music

During Year 3 children should gradually show a greater control and sophistication in selecting and combining sounds and musical phrases. They should aim to pay closer attention to the purpose of a composition, and make musical decisions that help to fulfil that purpose.

Children are given further opportunities to explore composing with music technology. They also continue to evaluate their own compositions in order to improve their work.

Listening with attention to detail

In Year 3 children continue to listen to recorded extracts of music, but rather than responding through movement the focus is now on providing verbal responses. Children are encouraged to find words and phrases to describe the music, building up their technical vocabulary, and to give reasons for their choices. Children also continue to listen to and evaluate their own compositions. They should start to find it easier to describe which bits of a composition are most successful, or which need more work, and why.

Using staff and other musical notations

Children continue to use rhythm grids to notate and perform music. They learn to read from one-line staves that indicate different pitches. The correct symbols for different note lengths are also introduced. This helps to lay the groundwork for working with traditional staff notation, which children are first introduced to later in the year.

Appreciating and understanding a wide range of music

Through the listening and performing activities in Year 3, children should begin to increase their understanding of different types of music, including the characteristics that identify different genres or styles.

Developing an understanding of the history of music

The key word here is 'understanding': children are not expected to learn the history of music. Instead, they need to understand that music has developed in different ways at different times, for a range of different purposes. During Year 3 this understanding can be developed primarily through the listening activities.

Medium-term planning Autumn 1

W	Activity summary	Curriculum objectives	Outcomes
1	Children review some of the songs they have learned in Years 1 and 2. They aim to sing more expressively, with a consideration of dynamics and articulation. Children plan an imaginary concert consisting of the songs they have learned during previous years. They should order the songs into an effective sequence.	• Learn to sing and to use their voices. • Listen to, review and evaluate music.	• Can recall songs learned during previous years. • Can think about how to order a concert effectively.
2	Children are given a selection of animal pictures. They listen to a few extracts from Saint-Saëns' *Carnival of the Animals*, and match up the pictures to the extracts. Encourage children to explain and evaluate their decisions by talking about different features of the music (instruments, tempo, mood and so on).	• Listen to, review and evaluate music. • Understand and explore the inter-related dimensions.	• Can describe some of the features of a piece of music.
3	Children develop an inner sense of pulse through stop/start singing games. Similar to Year 2, Spring 1, Week 4, stop/start singing games involve singing some of the lines of a song silently in your head. Begin with short, simple examples, including songs the children already know. Make the pulse obvious by tapping it clearly during the silent sections. As children gain in confidence, work with longer silent sections and remove the pulse.	• Learn to sing and to use their voices.	• Can remain quiet, but still keep a sense of pulse, in certain passages of a song.
4	Children play from rhythm grids where the dots have been swapped for conventional note lengths (for example, minims, crotchets and quavers). They compose their own rhythm patterns and notate these with rhythm grids, using different note lengths.	• Understand and explore how music is created using appropriate musical notations. • Understand and explore the inter-related dimensions: duration.	• Can create rhythm grids that use conventional note lengths.
5	Children swap their rhythm grids from the previous week and perform each other's patterns. Children explore playing the patterns on different instruments. In small groups, children order their patterns into an effective sequence to create a short piece. They rehearse this piece and perform it to the rest of the class.	• Understand and explore how music is created using appropriate musical notations. • Perform music.	• Can perform from rhythm grids that use conventional note lengths.
6	Review any work from the half term that might require further consolidation. Consider combining some or all of the activities that have been covered during this half term into a whole-class performance or presentation.		

Notes:
Visit the Scholastic website (www.scholastic.co.uk/100music) to find a sample lesson covering week 4's work on playing using simple rhythm grids.

MSCHOLASTIC

Medium-term planning Autumn 2

W	Activity summary	Curriculum objectives	Outcomes
1	Children sing or play short melodies from simple pitch notation (one-line staves indicating low, middle and high). Children compose their own melodies and use one-line staves to notate them.	• Understand and explore how music is created using appropriate musical notations. • Understand and explore the inter-related dimensions: pitch and duration.	• Can compose and notate short melodies using one-line staves.
2	Children put together a wallchart with a timeline from around AD500 to the present day. They divide the chart into sections to indicate the major periods of Western music. Each time children listen to a piece of music over the course of Key Stage 2, they add it to the chart. During this lesson children could start to fill in the wallchart by adding some famous composers, as well as any major events they have already studied in their history lessons.	• Listen to, review and evaluate music.	• Can begin to develop a sense of the history of Western music.
3	Children compose pieces using music technology (for example, a computer program such as *GarageBand*). They use the samples provided and focus on structuring them effectively into a complete piece. Similar to Year 2, Autumn 2, Week 4, this activity could include discussion as to what makes a musically satisfying and coherent structure.	• Use technology appropriately. • Create and compose music.	• Can utilise music technology to create an appropriate structure for a piece.
4	Similar to Year 2, Autumn 2, Week 1, children compose music to accompany a poem or story. This time, they focus on creating a musical motif for the main character. Having created a motif, children explore different ways of playing it (using different instruments or vocal sounds) to capture the character's personality. They should find ways to vary the motif to match the character's different actions or moods within the poem or story.	• Create and compose music. • Understand and explore the inter-related dimensions.	• Can compose and vary a motif to represent different situations or moods.
5	Children continue their work from the previous week. Using the motif (and its variations), they compose a piece to accompany a narration of the poem or story. Children should refine their pieces through rehearsal, performance and evaluation.	• Create and compose music. • Perform music.	• Can compose and perform a piece that makes use of a repeating motif.
6	Review any work from the half term that might require further consolidation. Consider combining some or all of the activities that have been covered during this half term into a whole-class performance or presentation.		

Notes:
Visit the Scholastic website (www.scholastic.co.uk/100music) to find a sample lesson covering week 4's work on composing music to accompany a poem or story.

Medium-term planning Spring 1

W	Activity summary	Curriculum objectives	Outcomes
1	Children use the natural rhythms of words to compose rhythmic ostinatos (for example, cat-er-pil-lar but-ter-fly, cat-er-pil-lar but-ter-fly). Children gradually layer up these ostinatos, performing them simultaneously. (For example, everyone in a group starts by playing the same pattern. The group then splits in half, each half playing a different pattern while maintaining a steady pulse.) This activity can be used to explore the concept of texture.	• Create and compose music. • Perform music. • Understand and explore the inter-related dimensions: duration and texture.	• Can compose simple rhythmic ostinatos. • Can hold a steady part against a contrasting rhythm.
2	Children continue their work from the previous week, trying to increase the number of layers (for example, splitting the group into three different parts). Children could also create more complex ostinatos by using different vocal and instrumental sounds.	• Create and compose music. • Perform music.	• Can compose more complex rhythmic ostinatos. • Can hold a steady part against one or more contrasting rhythms.
3	Children listen to an extract from Ravel's orchestration of Mussorgsky's *Pictures at an Exhibition*. Children respond to the extract by drawing or painting a picture that they feel is representative of the piece. Children compare their pictures to the original painting that inspired Mussorgsky's music. They discuss their work: which pictures best capture the character of the music, and why?	• Listen to, review and evaluate music.	• Can create a picture that is representative of a piece of music. • Can share and evaluate work.
4	Children review some of the songs they have learned so far. They aim to sing more expressively, with a consideration of dynamics, articulation and diction. Provide opportunities for small groups or soloists to sing certain sections of the songs.	• Learn to sing and to use their voices.	• Can sing expressively, with contrasting dynamics or articulation. • Can sing solo or in a small group.
5	Children learn a call-and-response song, where you sing a line (the 'call') and the children copy it (the 'response'). To make this harder, you could mix up the order of the calls, so children are not sure which one is coming next. Children could also take turns to lead the song by singing the calls themselves.	• Learn to sing and to use their voices.	• Can sing a call-and-response song.
6	Review any work from the half term that might require further consolidation. Consider combining some or all of the activities that have been covered during this half term into a whole-class performance or presentation.		

■SCHOLASTIC

Medium-term planning Spring 2

W	Activity summary	Curriculum objectives	Outcomes
1	Continuing their work from Year 3, Autumn 2, Week 1, children compose three-note melodies (high, middle and low) that make use of different note lengths (for example, minims, crotchets and quavers). Children notate the melodies using one-line staves that include barlines. Children could create accompaniments for their melodies by adding drones or rhythmic ostinatos.	• Create and compose music. • Understand and explore how music is created using appropriate musical notations.	• Can compose and notate short melodies using one-line staves.
2	Children continue their work from the previous week. In small groups, they share and combine their melodies to build up longer compositions. Children rehearse and perform their pieces to the rest of the class.	• Create and compose music. • Perform music.	• Can perform melodies notated on one-line staves.
3	Explain the inter-related dimensions. Ask the children to review them (most of them will already have been covered to some extent). Children then have to find ways to illustrate each dimension musically (for example, by singing a song quickly then slowly to illustrate tempo, or by playing a piece quietly then loudly to illustrate dynamics).	• Understand and explore inter-related dimensions.	• Can understand and demonstrate the inter-related dimensions.
4	Children sit facing each other in pairs, each with an instrument. They have a musical conversation on their instruments, each child gauging when it is their turn to play. Encourage children to respond musically to each other, rather than just playing anything. This could include elements of call and response (for example, one child plays a phrase and the other tries to copy it). Children could also try playing with opposites (for example, one child plays loudly, so the other plays quietly).	• Create and compose music. • Have the opportunity to learn a musical instrument.	• Can perform in dialogue with someone else, responding to them musically.
5	Children learn a simple ensemble piece (where there are a number of different layers to the piece, played on different instruments). While the piece should primarily be taught by ear, this could be a good opportunity to introduce children to reading simple staff notation. (For example, children could learn their parts and then compare what they have learned to how it is notated.)	• Understand and explore how music is created using appropriate musical notations. • Have the opportunity to learn a musical instrument.	• Can perform in an ensemble piece. • Can begin to read staff notation.
6	Review any work from the half term that might require further consolidation. Consider combining some or all of the activities that have been covered during this half term into a whole-class performance or presentation.		

Notes:
Visit the Scholastic website (www.scholastic.co.uk/100music) to find a sample lesson covering week 1's work on composing three-note melodies.

YEAR 3

Medium-term planning Summer 1

W	Activity summary	Curriculum objectives	Outcomes
1	Similar to Year 2, Summer 1, Week 4, children use the rhythms of a rhyme or chant as a stimulus for creating ostinatos. These ostinatos could be rhythmic or melodic. In groups, children combine some of their ostinatos to create a multi-layered piece. For example, this could consist of three layers: a melodic ostinato, a rhythmic ostinato, and the spoken rhyme or chant.	• Understand and explore the inter-related dimensions: duration, pitch and texture. • Have the opportunity to learn a musical instrument.	• Can maintain a rhythmic or melodic ostinato against a contrasting part.
2	Children continue their work from the previous week, rehearsing and performing their pieces. Children evaluate each other's performances. If there is time, they could make improvements to their pieces based on the feedback they received. Notate or record the ostinatos as a record for future use (see week 5).	• Perform music. • Listen to, review and evaluate music.	• Can maintain a rhythmic or melodic ostinato against a contrasting part. • Can improve their work through rehearsal and evaluation.
3	Children listen to a variety of extracts from contrasting styles or genres. In pairs, they answer simple questions about different features of the music (for example: 'Are there voices?' or 'Is this music fast or slow?'). Children discuss their responses with the rest of the class. This activity could be used to build up an understanding of the characteristics of certain styles of music.	• Listen to, review and evaluate music. • Understand and explore the inter-related dimensions.	• Can identify different features of a piece of music through listening.
4	Children add simple rhythmic accompaniments to their singing. Use a song that the class knows well. Start by adding simple rhythmic actions (for example, clapping or stamping on the beat). Then try combining different actions (for example, clapping on beat 1 and clicking on beat 3). Children who are confident with this could try adding very simple rhythmic ostinatos on percussion instruments.	• Learn to sing and to use their voices.	• Can sing and perform a simple rhythmic accompaniment at the same time.
5	Children review their ostinato patterns from weeks 1 and 2. They use an app (for example, *Music Mike Create*) or computer program (for example, *GarageBand*) to record some of the ostinatos and combine them together to create a new piece.	• Use technology appropriately. • Create and compose music.	• Can use technology to record samples and recombine them into a new piece.
6	Review any work from the half term that might require further consolidation. Consider combining some or all of the activities that have been covered during this half term into a whole-class performance or presentation.		

Medium-term planning Summer 2

W	Activity summary	Curriculum objectives	Outcomes
1	In groups, children create their own musical notation, inventing symbols to represent different sounds or elements (pitch, rhythm, dynamics, and so on). They use the symbols to compose and notate short pieces.	• Understand and explore how music is created using appropriate musical notations. • Create and compose music.	• Can invent appropriate symbols to represent different sounds and use these to notate a short piece.
2	Continuing their work from the previous week, each group swaps their score with another group's and tries to perform from it. These performances can be used to evaluate the effectiveness of the notation. *Did the performance sound like it was supposed to? If not, how can the notation be improved?* If there is time, children try to improve their scores based on the feedback received.	• Understand and explore how music is created using appropriate musical notations. • Perform music. • Listen to, review and evaluate music.	• Can perform from graphic notation. • Can evaluate and improve their work.
3	Children compose a piece to represent a particular mood or atmosphere. This could include discussion about how the inter-related dimensions can be used to represent different moods (for example, a fast tempo for 'happy' and a slow tempo for 'sad').	• Create and compose music. • Understand and explore the inter-related dimensions.	• Can compose music that evokes a particular mood or atmosphere.
4	Continuing their work from the previous week, children refine, rehearse and perform their pieces. Children evaluate each other's compositions: *How successful were they in capturing a particular mood, and why? How could they be improved?*	• Perform music. • Listen to, review and evaluate music.	• Can compose music that evokes a particular mood or atmosphere. • Can evaluate and improve their work.
5 & 6	Review any work from the half term that might require further consolidation. Children rehearse performances of some of the songs, pieces or compositions that have been learned or created during the year. These are presented in an end-of-year showcase or concert.	• Perform music.	• Can rehearse and perform music to a high standard.

Year 3 Background knowledge

Listening to a wide range of music

Teachers should aim to introduce children to a variety of different styles and genres of music throughout the course of Key Stage 2. A broad and balanced mix should include music that is relevant to the cultures of the children, as well as the interests and enthusiasms of the class and their teacher. While listening activities are the most obvious place to introduce a wider range of music, opportunities should be taken in other instances as well. For example, at the start of an activity where children have to compose a piece to a story or poem, the teacher could play a programmatic work such as Berlioz's Symphonie fantastique. At the start of an activity where children have to perform rhythmic ostinatos, the teacher could play some of Steve Reich's music.

Working with the inter-related dimensions

No music is one-dimensional; every piece will have its own distinctive combination of pitches, durations, dynamics, timbres and so on. This means that while certain activities may focus on one particular dimension, children should also develop an understanding of how the dimensions work together holistically.

Throughout the course of the year, encourage children to incorporate more of the dimensions into their music making more often. This can help to improve the musicality of their work. For example, including dynamics in a song can help to make it sound more musical. If a child has composed a melody where all the notes are the same length, encourage them to think about rhythm as well in order to take their work to the next level.

Using one-line staves

A one-line stave can be used to work with any combination of three notes. The low note sits below the line, the middle note on the line, and the high note above the line. Here is an example:

This one-line stave incorporates different note lengths as well. The first note is a minim (two beats long), the second note a crotchet (one beat long) and the third note a quaver (half a beat long). There are four beats in each bar: this is indicated by the time signature and barlines (see the 'Background knowledge' section for Year 1 for a very brief explanation of time signatures and bars).

Exploring texture

Various activities in this year require children to work with more than one layer in a piece (for example, where two groups are playing different rhythms at the same time, creating two layers). These activities can be used to explore the concept of texture (essentially, how many layers there are in a piece and how they interact). This can be one of the hardest dimensions to understand, although like any concept it can be simplified. A good way to start is by thinking about 'thin' and 'thick' textures. (One instrument playing by itself is a 'thin' texture; lots of instruments playing different things at the same time is a 'thick' texture.)

Year 4 Long-term planning

Year 4 is based on the same subject content as Year 3, which states that children should be taught to:

- Play and perform in solo and ensemble contexts, using their voices and playing musical instruments with increasing accuracy, fluency, control and expression.
- Improvise and compose music for a range of purposes using the inter-related dimensions of music.
- Listen with attention to detail and recall sounds with increasing aural memory.
- Use and understand staff and other musical notations.
- Appreciate and understand a wide range of high-quality live and recorded music drawn from different traditions and from great composers and musicians.
- Develop an understanding of the history of music.

The medium-term plans that follow comprise six half-termly units that provide children with opportunities to progress with music making across the six areas mentioned above. The activity summaries for each half term, together with the background knowledge provided at the end of the year, should be sufficient in providing the support that is required for teachers to design lesson plans for their respective classes.

As with previous years, teachers will want to use these plans flexibly and adapt them to their requirements. They will want to think about prioritising certain activities, while at the same time maintaining a broad and balanced curriculum. Up to this point, most activities will have relied upon typical classroom instruments (such as percussion and keyboards). Now would be a good time to start providing opportunities for children to work with other musical instruments. This may involve whole-class tuition as part of a Wider Opportunities-type scheme. Additionally, some children will be starting to learn instruments as an extra-curricular activity. They should be actively encouraged to use those instruments in the classroom, as a way of extending the range of sounds that are available for composing and performing activities.

Year 4 focuses primarily on the following activities:

- Listening to and evaluating music, including the children's own compositions.
- Reviewing and building the class' repertoire of songs; learning to sing in two-part harmony.
- Playing from and composing with notation, including one-line staves and staff notation.
- Carrying out various composition activities, some of which use music technology.
- Cementing an understanding of the inter-related dimensions.
- Playing instruments in a variety of contexts.

Overview of progression in Year 4

In Year 4 children will consolidate and build on the skills and understanding covered in Year 3. Some of the activities use similar starting points to those provided in previous years, but with the aim of taking the learning further and deeper.

Based on the subject content for Key Stage 2 (outlined on the previous page), progression in Year 4 can be summarised as follows:

Performing in solo and ensemble contexts

As with previous years, children are given various opportunities to perform both vocal and instrumental music. Children learn to sing in two-part harmony, and concentrate on refining their singing skills by improving their diction and expression. Children continue to perform more complex pieces that include a number of different layers. They should aim for greater accuracy and fluency in their playing.

Improvising and composing music

During Year 4 children should continue to show a greater control and sophistication in selecting and combining sounds and musical phrases. They should aim to pay closer attention to the purpose of a composition, and make musical decisions that help to fulfil that purpose.

Children are given further opportunities to explore composing with music technology. They also continue to evaluate their own compositions in order to improve their work.

Listening with attention to detail

In Year 4 children continue to listen to recorded extracts of music and analyse them through verbal responses. Children should continue to build up their technical vocabulary in order to describe the music they hear. They also continue to listen to and evaluate their own compositions. They should find it easier to describe which bits of a composition are most successful, or which need more work, and why.

Using staff and other notations

Children continue to compose with one-line staves that indicate both pitch and rhythm. They also study the staff notation for an ensemble piece they have learned to play, which allows them to become more familiar with reading this type of notation.

Appreciating and understanding a wide range of music

Through the listening and performing activities in Year 4, children should continue to increase their understanding of different types of music, including the characteristics that identify different genres or styles.

Developing an understanding of the history of music

Children continue to develop a familiarity with the history of music. They use the musical-timeline wallchart that was introduced in Year 3 to consolidate their understanding of how music has changed over time. They begin to recognise the musical differences between pieces from contrasting periods.

Medium-term planning Autumn 1

W	Activity summary	Curriculum objectives	Outcomes
1	Similar to Year 3, Summer 1, Week 1, children use the rhythms of a rhyme or chant as a stimulus for creating ostinatos. These ostinatos could be rhythmic or melodic, and incorporate a variety of instrumental and vocal sounds. In groups, children combine their ostinatos to create a multi-layered piece.	• Understand and explore the inter-related dimensions: duration, pitch and texture. • Have the opportunity to learn a musical instrument.	• Can maintain a rhythmic or melodic ostinato against one or more contrasting parts.
2	Children continue their work from the previous week, rehearsing and performing their pieces. They try playing their pieces at different tempos (for example, slowly then quickly) while always maintaining a steady pulse. Children evaluate each other's performances. If there is time, they could make improvements to their pieces based on the feedback they received.	• Perform music. • Listen to, review and evaluate music.	• Can maintain a rhythmic or melodic ostinato against one or more contrasting parts. • Can improve their work through rehearsal and evaluation.
3	Children try to identify an instrument playing a solo part in a recorded piece (for example, a guitar solo in a pop song or a piano solo in a concerto). They have a selection of pictures and names to choose from. Children try to find words to describe the different timbres of the instruments (using words such as 'soft', 'warm', 'rough' and so on).	• Listen to, review and evaluate music. • Understand and explore the inter-related dimensions: timbre.	• Can identify certain instruments, if not by name then by family (such as brass, woodwind, strings or percussion). • Can describe different instrumental timbres.
4	Children learn to sing in two-part harmony. Learning a round can be a good way to start; alternatively, children could add a very simple ostinato part to a song they already know well. If children feel confident with this, they could go on to learn a simple two-part song.	• Learn to sing and to use their voices.	• Can maintain a vocal part against a contrasting one.
5	Children listen to a selection of pieces with descriptive titles (for example, Dvorak's *The Water Goblin* or Vaughan Williams' *The Lark Ascending*). They discuss how the music evokes the title, referring to the instruments and inter-related dimensions. Children listen to another descriptive piece (where they don't know the title) and invent their own title and story to accompany it. They compare their titles with the composer's original.	• Listen to, review and evaluate music. • Understand and explore the inter-related dimensions.	• Can explain how music evokes certain moods, characters or events.
6	Review any work from the half term that might require further consolidation. Consider combining some or all of the activities that have been covered during this half term into a whole-class performance or presentation.		

Notes:
Visit the Scholastic website (www.scholastic.co.uk/100music) to find a sample lesson covering week 1's work on using rhythms as a stimulus for creating ostinatos.

Medium-term planning Autumn 2

W	Activity summary	Curriculum objectives	Outcomes
1	Children compose three-note melodies (high, middle and low) and notate them using one-line staves. This is similar to Year 3, Spring 2, Week 1, except now children should aim to create interesting rhythms for their melodies by using a combination of different note lengths and rests.	• Understand and explore how music is created using appropriate musical notations. • Create and compose music.	• Can compose and notate short melodies using one-line staves.
2	Children continue their work from the previous week. In small groups, they share and combine their melodies to build up longer compositions. Children rehearse and perform their pieces to the rest of the class.	• Create and compose music. • Perform music.	• Can perform melodies notated on one-line staves.
3	Children listen to two contrasting pieces of music, each one from a different period of musical history. They make a list of the similarities and differences between the two pieces. Explain which of the musical features are typical for each period, and provide some information about the composer and context of the pieces.	• Listen to, review and evaluate music.	• Can compare and contrast two pieces of music.
4	Children compose pieces using music technology (for example, a computer program such as *GarageBand*). They use the samples provided and focus on structuring them effectively into a complete piece. This is similar to Year 3, Autumn 2, Week 3, although children should now aim to be more discerning in selecting and combining samples to create a piece that has a clear structure.	• Use technology appropriately. • Create and compose music. • Understand and explore the inter-related dimensions: structure.	• Can utilise music technology to create an appropriate structure for a piece.
5	Children continue the previous week's work. They refine their pieces and pay attention to aspects such as the tempo and dynamics. Children listen to and evaluate each other's compositions.	• Use technology appropriately. • Create and compose music.	• Can use music software to edit and refine a composition. • Can share and evaluate work.
6	Review any work from the half term that might require further consolidation. Consider combining some or all of the activities that have been covered during this half term into a whole-class performance or presentation.		

Medium-term planning Spring 1

W	Activity summary	Curriculum objectives	Outcomes
1	In groups, children compose pieces that are built from a number of different layers (for example, a rhythmic ostinato for the first layer, a melody for the second layer and a drone for the last layer). Children practise performing their pieces, playing all of the layers simultaneously while maintaining a steady pulse. They find a way to notate or record their layers for use in next week's lesson.	• Create and compose music. • Perform music.	• Can compose and perform a piece with more than one layer.
2	Children continue their work from the previous week. They mix around the groups to try combining layers in different combinations. They evaluate which layers work best together and why, developing an understanding of what makes an effective accompaniment.	• Create and compose music. • Listen to, review and evaluate music.	• Can compose and perform a piece with more than one layer. • Can share and evaluate work.
3	Children listen to extracts of music associated with particular occasions or events (for example, fanfares, Christmas carols or football chants). They consider where they might hear such music, and what it is about the music that makes it suitable for the occasion or event. If time is available, children could learn to sing or play a short piece that has been composed for a specific event.	• Listen to, review and evaluate music.	• Can explain why music is suited to a particular occasion or event.
4	Children improve their confidence with singing in two-part harmony, building on the work done in Year 4, Autumn 1, Week 4. This could involve learning a new two-part song.	• Learn to sing and to use their voices.	• Can maintain a vocal part against a contrasting one.
5	Children refine their singing skills by concentrating on their expression and diction. They practise singing different sections of a song with contrasting dynamics. They learn tongue twisters and practise saying (or singing) these at faster and faster tempos.	• Learn to sing and to use their voices.	• Can sing expressively and with clear diction.
6	Review any work from the half term that might require further consolidation. Consider combining some or all of the activities that have been covered during this half term into a whole-class performance or presentation.		

Notes:
Visit the Scholastic website (www.scholastic.co.uk/100music) to find a sample lesson covering week 1's work on composing pieces built from a number of different layers.

Medium-term planning Spring 2

W	Activity summary	Curriculum objectives	Outcomes
1	Similar to Year 4, Autumn 2, Week 1, children compose and notate a melody using a one-line stave. They aim to use a variety of note lengths, making sure that each bar adds up to the correct number of beats. Children compose a rhythmic line to accompany their melody (for example, a tambourine part), which they can also notate on a one-line stave.	• Understand and explore how music is created using appropriate musical notations. • Create and compose music.	• Can compose and notate short melodies using one-line staves.
2	Children continue their work from the previous week. They rehearse and perform their melodies. If time is available, children could swap their melodies and try to perform from each other's notations.	• Understand and explore how music is created using appropriate musical notations. • Perform music.	• Can perform melodies notated on one-line staves.
3	Children use music technology to compose a soundscape on a particular theme (for example, a rainforest or horror-film soundscape). Children start by recording a variety of vocal, instrumental and everyday sounds. They use effects to manipulate the sounds so they fit the theme of the soundscape. Children then combine and order their sounds into a complete soundscape.	• Use technology appropriately. • Create and compose music.	• Can use technology to record and manipulate sounds.
4	Children continue their work from the previous week, refining and sharing their compositions. Children evaluate the soundscapes, deciding which sounds are the most effective and discussing how to improve the sounds that are not so successful.	• Use technology appropriately. • Listen to, review and evaluate music.	• Can compose with technology. • Can share and evaluate work.
5	Children sit facing each other in pairs, each with an instrument. They have a musical conversation on their instruments, each child gauging when it is their turn to play. Encourage children to respond musically to each other, rather than just playing anything. This could include elements of call and response (for example, one child plays a phrase and the other tries to copy it). Children could also try playing with opposites (for example, one child plays loudly, so the other plays quietly).	• Create and compose music. • Have the opportunity to learn a musical instrument.	• Can perform in dialogue with someone else, responding to them musically.
6	Review any work from the half term that might require further consolidation. Consider combining some or all of the activities that have been covered during this half term into a whole-class performance or presentation.		

Medium-term planning Summer 1

W	Activity summary	Curriculum objectives	Outcomes
1	Similar to Year 3, Spring 2, Week 5, children learn a simple ensemble piece (where there are a number of different layers to the piece, played on different instruments). While the piece should primarily be learned by ear, this could be a good opportunity for children to become more familiar with reading simple staff notation. For example, once children have learned their parts, they could compare what they have learned to how it is notated. Encourage children to use any instruments they have been learning as an extra-curricular activity.	• Understand and explore how music is created using appropriate musical notations. • Have the opportunity to learn a musical instrument.	• Can perform in an ensemble piece. • Can begin to read staff notation.
2	Children continue to rehearse the piece from the previous week. They aim for greater accuracy, control and expression in their playing. Having become more familiar with the piece, children spend a bit more time understanding how it is notated.	• Understand and explore how music is created using appropriate musical notations. • Have the opportunity to learn a musical instrument.	• Can perform in an ensemble piece. • Can begin to read staff notation.
3	In small groups, children listen to three short extracts of music and decide which one they think is the odd one out and why. Each group shares their reasoning with the rest of the class. The activity is repeated with a different selection of extracts. This activity could be used to review the inter-related dimensions. For example: *which extract is the odd one out in terms of the dynamics/ instrumentation/texture, and so on?*	• Listen to, review and evaluate music. • Understand and explore the inter-related dimensions.	• Can compare and contrast pieces of music.
4	Similar to Year 2, Summer 1, Week 4, children use the rhythms of a rhyme or chant as a stimulus for creating ostinatos. These ostinatos could be rhythmic or melodic. In groups, children combine some of their ostinatos to create a multi-layered piece. They experiment with different textures and structures, where individual parts drop in and out at different times.	• Understand and explore the inter-related dimensions: texture and structure. • Create and compose music.	• Can maintain a rhythmic or melodic ostinato against a contrasting part.
5	Children rehearse and then notate their pieces from the previous week, using staff, grid or graphic notation (or a combination of all three). Children swap their notations and try to perform each other's pieces. If there is time, they assess how effective the notation is and clarify any misunderstandings about how to read it.	• Understand and explore how music is created using appropriate musical notations. • Perform music.	• Can maintain a rhythmic or melodic ostinato against a contrasting part. • Can compose and perform using notation.
6	Review any work from the half term that might require further consolidation. Consider combining some or all of the activities that have been covered during this half term into a whole-class performance or presentation.		

YEAR 4

Medium-term planning Summer 2

W	Activity summary	Curriculum objectives	Outcomes
1	Children review the musical-timeline wallchart that they have been adding to since Year 3 (see Year 3, Autumn 2, Week 2). They look for gaps in the chart and listen to some pieces from periods that have not yet been covered. They discuss the musical features of these pieces and learn about their composers.	• Listen to, review and evaluate music.	• Can understand how music has developed over time.
2	Children review some of the action songs they have learned so far. They pick one of the songs and try to make the actions more complex, mixing some body percussion into the sequence. Children who are confident with this could try adding very simple rhythmic ostinatos on percussion instruments.	• Learn to sing and to use their voices.	• Can sing and perform a simple rhythmic accompaniment at the same time.
3	Children review the inter-related dimensions by composing variations on a short melody. Each variation should highlight a different dimension (for example, one variation could make use of a range of dynamics; another could alter the rhythms of the melody).	• Create and compose music. • Explore and understand the inter-related dimensions.	• Can make use of all of the dimensions in a composition.
4	Children continue their work from the previous week. They refine, rehearse and perform their variations. Children listen to each other's variations and have to guess which dimensions are being highlighted. They explain their decisions using musical vocabulary.	• Listen to, review and evaluate music. • Explore and understand the inter-related dimensions.	• Can identify the different dimensions in a composition.
5 & 6	Review any work from the half term that might require further consolidation. Children rehearse performances of some of the songs, pieces or compositions that have been learned or created during the year. These are presented in an end-of-year showcase or concert.	• Perform music.	• Can rehearse and perform music to a high standard.

Year 4 Background knowledge

Singing in two-part harmony

Children often find singing in two parts a challenge, although it is an activity that can be introduced very simply. A good way to start is by learning a well-known round, such as 'Row, Row, Row Your Boat'. Alternatively, children could add a drone or simple ostinato part to a song they already know well. If there are any confident singers in the class, they should be evenly split between the two parts.

Working with layers of sound

Children are expected to perform and compose more pieces this year that consist of two or more layers. For composition work, children should aim to compose layers that contrast but also complement each other well. In this case, less is often more: if too many of the layers are busy and complicated, the piece will sound very messy. Encourage children to keep their layers simple, and to tweak them so they fit together well.

Differentiation

Differentiation arguably becomes more difficult in music as children get older, because the gap widens between the children who play music as an extra-curricular activity and the rest of the class. In Key Stage 2, as children start to have instrumental lessons, this is most likely to become an issue in performance or notation-based activities.

To help counteract this, whenever teachers introduce a new song or piece to the class they should aim to make sure there is at least one easy part and one harder part. This may require teachers to adapt or invent new parts, such as a very simple ostinato rhythm or a more complex countermelody. Children who are more confident should also be encouraged to help teach and mentor children who are less experienced.

Exploring timbre

The activity in Autumn 1 Week 3 consciously introduces the concept of 'timbre' for the first time. Along with texture, this can be one of the hardest of the inter-related dimensions to understand. Timbre can be thought of as the sound quality of a particular instrument or voice: it is the aspect of the instrument or voice that makes it sound different to another one. (For example, when a guitar and violin play the same note at the same volume, you can still tell the difference between the two instruments. This is because they have different timbres.)

The concept can be explained simply to children as 'the type of sound an instrument makes'. Timbre is generally referred to with descriptive words such as 'rough', 'smooth', 'bright', 'breathy' and so on.

Reading staff notation

Staff notation may seem complicated, but it is not too dissimilar to one-line staves. The most obvious difference is that the stave consists of five lines rather than one. Here is a short example:

Each line or space on the stave represents a different pitch. To help children when they are first learning to read staff notation, write the letter name of each note underneath it (as in the example above).

Year 5 Long-term planning

Year 5 is based on the same subject content as Year 4, which states that children should be taught to:

- Play and perform in solo and ensemble contexts, using their voices and playing musical instruments with increasing accuracy, fluency, control and expression.
- Improvise and compose music for a range of purposes using the inter-related dimensions of music.
- Listen with attention to detail and recall sounds with increasing aural memory.
- Use and understand staff and other musical notations.
- Appreciate and understand a wide range of high-quality live and recorded music drawn from different traditions and from great composers and musicians.
- Develop an understanding of the history of music.

The medium-term plans that follow comprise six half-termly units that provide children with opportunities to progress with music making across the six areas mentioned above. The activity summaries for each half term, together with the background knowledge provided at the end of the year, should be sufficient in providing the support that is required for teachers to design lesson plans for their respective classes.

Year 5 focuses primarily on the following activities:

- Listening to and evaluating music, including the children's own compositions.
- Reviewing and building the class' repertoire of songs.
- Playing from and composing with notation, including one-line staves and staff notation.
- Carrying out various composition activities, with a focus in this year on composing melodies.
- Cementing an understanding of the inter-related dimensions.
- Playing instruments in a variety of contexts.

Overview of progression in Year 5

In Year 5 children will consolidate and build on the skills and understanding covered in Year 4. Some of the activities use similar starting points to those provided in previous years, but with the aim of taking the learning further and deeper.

Based on the subject content for Key Stage 2 (outlined on the previous page), progression in Year 5 can be summarised as follows:

Performing in solo and ensemble contexts

As with previous years, children are given various opportunities to perform both vocal and instrumental music. They continue to practise singing in two-part harmony and aim to sing more expressively. Children continue to play more complex pieces that include a number of different layers. In particular they work on their melodic playing, learning to play melodies fluently and accurately.

Improvising and composing music

During Year 5 children should continue to show a greater control and sophistication in selecting and combining sounds and musical phrases. They develop their ability to compose effective melodies, and start to think about using harmony in their pieces.

Children are given further opportunities to explore composing with music technology. They also continue to evaluate their own compositions in order to improve their work.

Listening with attention to detail

In Year 5 children continue to listen to recorded extracts of music and analyse them through verbal responses. Children should continue to build up their technical vocabulary in order to describe the music they hear. They also continue to listen to and evaluate their own compositions. They should find it easier to describe which bits of a composition are most successful, or which need more work, and why.

Using staff and other notations

Children continue to develop their ability to perform from and compose with various types of notation, including one-line staves and staff notation.

Appreciating and understanding a wide range of music

Through the listening and performing activities in Year 5, children should continue to increase their understanding of different types of music, including the characteristics that identify different genres or styles.

Developing an understanding of the history of music

Children continue to develop a familiarity with the history of music. They consolidate their understanding of how music has changed over time, and recognise some of the musical differences between pieces from contrasting periods.

Medium-term planning Autumn 1

YEAR 5

W	Activity summary	Curriculum objectives	Outcomes
1	Children review selected songs from the previous year (including at least one song in two-part harmony). Encourage children to sing with a greater accuracy in pitch and rhythm. Vocal warm-ups can help with this. Children should also aim to sing more expressively, paying attention to their dynamics and articulation.	• Learn to sing and to use their voices.	• Can recall songs learned during the previous year. • Can sing with greater accuracy in pitch and rhythm.
2	Children develop group compositions based on a pentatonic (five-note) scale. They compose a number of complementary layers (for example, a melody accompanied by a rhythmic ostinato and drone). They make decisions about how to structure the piece and how to vary the texture (for example, by dropping different parts in and out).	• Create and compose music. • Understand and explore the inter-related dimensions.	• Can compose a piece based on a pentatonic scale.
3	Children continue their work from the previous week. They refine, rehearse and perform their pieces. Children evaluate each other's performances. If there is time, they could make improvements to their pieces based on the feedback they received.	• Create and compose music. • Perform music. • Listen to, review and evaluate music.	• Can perform a piece that uses a pentatonic scale. • Can improve their work through rehearsal and evaluation.
4	Children compare CD covers from different genres and styles. They discuss how the cover images 'sell' the music on the CD. Children listen to other extracts of music and produce their own CD covers to accompany them. This activity could be used to explore the history of music. For example, children could create CD covers for music from different periods. The covers could be used to explore some of the ways that music has changed over time.	• Listen to, review and evaluate music.	• Can use appropriate language to describe how an image reflects a particular type of music. • Can create a CD cover to match an extract of music.
5	Children learn a new two-part song. They continue to develop their ability to maintain a vocal part against a contrasting one.	• Learn to sing and to use their voices.	• Can maintain a vocal part against a contrasting one.
6	Review any work from the half term that might require further consolidation. Consider combining some or all of the activities that have been covered during this half term into a whole-class performance or presentation.		

Notes:
Visit the Scholastic website (www.scholastic.co.uk/100music) to find a sample lesson covering week 2's work on developing group compositions based on a pentatonic scale.

■SCHOLASTIC

Medium-term planning Autumn 2

W	Activity summary	Curriculum objectives	Outcomes
1	Children learn about simple techniques for composing and extending melodies (for example, repetition, variation, sequence and inversion). They use some of these techniques to write their own melodies. Encourage children to think about rhythm as well as pitch, and to use a combination of different note lengths and rests.	• Create and compose music.	• Can use simple techniques to extend a melody. • Can compose a melody that incorporates different note lengths and rests.
2	Children continue the previous week's work. They devise accompaniments for their melodies using drones, rhythmic ostinatos or simple chords. Children rehearse, perform and evaluate their pieces.	• Create and compose music. • Perform music.	• Can create an appropriate accompaniment for a melody.
3	As a whole-class ensemble, children learn to play a samba piece with simple syncopated rhythms and a number of different layers. Once they have learned their parts by ear, children attempt to notate their rhythms (either using rhythm grids or one-line staves).	• Perform music. • Understand and explore how music is created using appropriate musical notations.	• Can maintain a rhythmic ostinato against more than one contrasting part.
4	Building on weeks 1 and 2, and similar to Year 3, Autumn 2, Week 4, children invent a character (for example, a new superhero) and compose a motif that encapsulates their personality. Children explore different ways of playing and varying the motif to match the character in different situations or moods.	• Create and compose music. • Understand and explore the inter-related dimensions.	• Can compose and vary a motif to represent different situations or moods.
5	Children continue their work from the previous week. They create a rough storyboard that places their character in different situations. Using the motif (and its variations), they compose a piece that reflects the events in the storyboard. Children refine their pieces through rehearsal, performance and evaluation.	• Create and compose music. • Perform music. • Listen to, review and evaluate music.	• Can compose and perform a piece that makes use of a repeating motif.
6	Review any work from the half term that might require further consolidation. Consider combining some or all of the activities that have been covered during this half term into a whole-class performance or presentation.		

Medium-term planning Spring 1

W	Activity summary	Curriculum objectives	Outcomes
1	Children learn to sing a round (for example, 'Row, Row, Row your Boat' or similar). They then try to compose their own very simple, two-part rounds, to be played on instruments. This activity could make use of music technology. For example, children compose a short melody. They record it using an app or computer program. They play back the recording while simultaneously playing the melody on an instrument to create a round.	• Learn to sing and to use their voices. • Create and compose music. • Use technology appropriately.	• Can sing a round. • Can compose and perform a simple round.
2	Children continue their work from the previous week. They refine their rounds and practise performing them (either in pairs or using music technology as described above).	• Create and compose music. • Perform music.	• Can compose and perform a simple round.
3	Children listen to extracts of music from around the world. They describe some of the main differences between the extracts using musical vocabulary. Using a world map as an aid, they try to guess which countries the extracts are from and explain their reasons. This activity could be used to explore different instruments from around the world, using websites such as the Virtual Instrument Museum.	• Listen to, review and evaluate music.	• Can use appropriate language to describe the differences between extracts of music. • Can locate different types of world music on a map.
4	In groups, children compose a short song. Children could write the lyrics themselves (perhaps related to a relevant cross-curricular topic) or use the words from a poem. Children should focus on creating a catchy melody that is fun to sing. They could also add a simple accompaniment, such as a rhythmic ostinato or some basic chords.	• Create and compose music.	• Can compose a song.
5	Children continue their work from the previous week. They rehearse and perform their songs. The whole class then tries to learn one or more of the songs. Children take an active role in teaching their songs to each other.	• Create and compose music. • Perform music.	• Can perform a song as part of a small group. • Can take part in peer learning.
6	Review any work from the half term that might require further consolidation. Consider combining some or all of the activities that have been covered during this half term into a whole-class performance or presentation.		

Medium-term planning Spring 2

W	Activity summary	Curriculum objectives	Outcomes
1	Children compose a bass line to a simple melody that they know well (for example, a phrase from a song they have learned to sing). The bass line does not need to have a complicated rhythm (for example, it could just consist of minims), but children should pay attention to finding notes that sound right against the melody.	• Create and compose music.	• Can compose a bass line to accompany a melody.
2	Children continue their work from the previous week. They refine their bass lines and practise performing them as an accompaniment to their melodies.	• Create and compose music. • Perform music.	• Can compose and perform a bass line to accompany a melody.
3	Using keyboards, xylophones or glockenspiels, children practise playing simple, short melodies from one-line staves. Children who are confident with this could practise playing melodies from staff notation.	• Have the opportunity to learn a musical instrument. • Understand and explore how music is created using appropriate musical notation.	• Can play simple melodies from notation.
4	Improvise short phrases and sing them to the class. Children repeat each phrase in a call-and-response manner. Children then work in pairs or small groups to improvise their own call-and-response phrases. One child sings or plays a phrase and the others copy it. To extend this activity, children could also improvise their own responses (where the response does not have to be exactly the same as the call, although it should complement it).	• Learn to sing and to use their voices. • Perform music.	• Can repeat short musical phrases by ear. • Can improvise calls and responses.
5	Children work in small groups to develop short compositions based on the previous week's activity. The compositions should have a call-and-response structure and could be vocal or instrumental. Children rehearse and perform their pieces.	• Create and compose music.	• Can compose a piece with a call-and-response structure.
6	Review any work from the half term that might require further consolidation. Consider combining some or all of the activities that have been covered during this half term into a whole-class performance or presentation.		

Medium-term planning Summer 1

W	Activity summary	Curriculum objectives	Outcomes
1	Similar to Year 4, Autumn 1, Week 1, children use the rhythms of a rhyme or chant as a stimulus for creating melodic ostinatos based on a pentatonic scale. Children practise playing their ostinatos fluently. Once they are confident with this, they can compose small variations and add them into repetitions of the ostinato. Children could also add drones or simple chords to their ostinatos as an accompaniment.	• Create and compose music. • Have the opportunity to learn a musical instrument.	• Can compose melodic ostinatos using a pentatonic scale. • Can perform melodic ostinatos fluently.
2	Children continue their work from the previous week. They rehearse their ostinatos and perform them to the rest of the class.	• Perform music.	• Can perform melodic ostinatos fluently.
3	Children listen to a selection of extracts from different periods of history and attempt to place them in an appropriate position on the musical-timeline wallchart (see Year 3, Autumn 2, Week 2). They discuss the reasons for their choices using musical vocabulary. The teacher guides children towards the correct answers and supplies a bit of information about the composer of each extract.	• Listen to, review and evaluate music.	• Can begin to determine roughly when a piece of music was composed.
4	As a whole-class ensemble, children learn to play a simple folk song. Some children could sing or play the melody; others could play a rhythmic ostinato or an accompanying harmonic part (for example, a drone or some simple chords). If there is time, encourage children to swap parts.	• Have the opportunity to learn a musical instrument.	• Can perform as part of an ensemble.
5	Children learn a simple folk dance (for example, a ceilidh dance) and perform this to a folk tune. This activity could be used to learn about different types of folk music and dance from around Europe.	• Listen to, review and evaluate music.	• Can perform a folk dance in time to music.
6	Review any work from the half term that might require further consolidation. Consider combining some or all of the activities that have been covered during this half term into a whole-class performance or presentation.		

Notes:
Visit the Scholastic website (www.scholastic.co.uk/100music) to find a sample lesson covering week 1's work on using rhythms as a stimulus for creating a melodic ostinato based on a pentatonic scale.

Medium-term planning Summer 2

W	Activity summary	Curriculum objectives	Outcomes
1	Similar to Year 3, Summer 2, Week 1, children invent their own graphic notation, paying particular attention to finding ways to notate timbre and texture. They compose and notate short pieces using their own notation.	• Understand and explore how music is created using appropriate musical notations. • Create and compose music.	• Can invent appropriate symbols to represent different dimensions and use these to notate a short piece.
2	Children continue the previous week's work. They swap their pieces and perform from each other's scores. These performances can be used to evaluate the effectiveness of the notation. *Did the performance sound like it was supposed to? If not, how can the notation be improved?* If there is time, children try to improve their scores based on the feedback received.	• Understand and explore how music is created using appropriate musical notations. • Perform music.	• Can perform from graphic notation. • Can evaluate and improve their work.
3	As a whole-class ensemble, children improvise music in response to a series of paintings that evoke different atmospheres. This could involve discussion as to how the paintings can best be represented through music. This activity could be free improvisation (where children play anything they like) or more structured (for example, restricted to a particular scale, rhythm or motif). Children could make use of music technology to add appropriate sound effects.	• Have the opportunity to learn a musical instrument. • Use technology appropriately.	• Can improvise music to match a particular mood.
4	Children review some of the songs learned in previous terms or years. Where appropriate the teacher increases the complexity of these songs (for example, by adding a harmony part or more complicated actions). Children should be given the opportunity to sing in small groups or on their own if they wish.	• Learn to sing and to use their voices.	• Can sing more complex songs.
5 & 6	Review any work from the half term that might require further consolidation. Children rehearse performances of some of the songs, pieces or compositions that have been learned or created during the year. These are presented in an end-of-year showcase or concert.	• Perform music.	• Can rehearse and perform music to a high standard.

Year 5 Background knowledge

Working with pentatonic scales

As children become more confident composers they can work with a wider range of notes. A couple of activities in Year 5 introduce pentatonic scales for the first time. A pentatonic scale is simply a sequence of five notes. At its simplest, this means that children could just work with the notes C, D, E, F and G; those who are more confident could use a pentatonic scale that includes gaps between some of the notes, such as this one:

When children are working with a limited selection of notes it can be helpful to remove the keys that are not needed (on a glockenspiel or xylophone) or to sticker the keys that are needed (on a piano or keyboard).

Extending melodies

A number of the activities in Year 5 focus on writing effective melodies. While children may find it quite easy to come up with initial ideas, they will often struggle to extend those ideas into longer, coherent melodies. There are a number of simple composition techniques that can help here, which include:

- Repetition: where the phrase is repeated exactly.
- Variation: where the phrase is repeated but with a slight variation (for example, the melody goes up at the end rather than down).
- Sequence: where the phrase is repeated exactly but at a different pitch.
- Inversion: where the melody is repeated upside down (for example, a rising phrase becomes a falling one).

Children can also vary aspects such as the dynamics and articulation to add interest to their melodies.

As children gradually compose longer and more complex pieces they will find it increasingly helpful to be able to record their ideas so they do not forget them. Children who are more confident with notation may be able to jot down their ideas; others may find it easier to use audio recorders. Notation software can also be useful in allowing students to play back their ideas so they can hear exactly what they sound like.

Composing rounds

The activity in Spring 1, Weeks 1 and 2 requires children to compose a very simple round. A round is a melody that is heard with itself but out of time. One group starts singing the melody. A second group waits for a short number of beats and then begins the melody as well (so they sing exactly the same thing but just a bit later than the first group). Here is an example of the start of a round:

The trick is to write a melody that creates a nice harmony when it is heard against itself. This may require quite a lot of trial and error; encourage children to listen critically to their rounds, and steer them towards creating intervals of a third where possible.

Year 6 Long-term planning

Year 6 is based on the same subject content as Year 5, which states that children should be taught to:

- Play and perform in solo and ensemble contexts, using their voices and playing musical instruments with increasing accuracy, fluency, control and expression.
- Improvise and compose music for a range of purposes using the inter-related dimensions of music.
- Listen with attention to detail and recall sounds with increasing aural memory.
- Use and understand staff and other musical notations.
- Appreciate and understand a wide range of high-quality live and recorded music drawn from different traditions and from great composers and musicians.
- Develop an understanding of the history of music.

The medium-term plans that follow comprise six half-termly units that provide children with opportunities to progress with music making across the six areas mentioned above. The activity summaries for each half term, together with the background knowledge provided at the end of the year, should be sufficient in providing the support that is required for teachers to design lesson plans for their respective classes.

Year 6 focuses primarily on the following activities:

- Listening to and evaluating music, including the children's own compositions.
- Reviewing and building the class' repertoire of songs.
- Playing from and composing with notation, including one-line staves and staff notation.
- Carrying out various composition activities.
- Cementing an understanding of the inter-related dimensions.
- Playing instruments in a variety of contexts.

Overview of progression in Year 6

In Year 6 children will consolidate and build on the skills and understanding covered in Year 5. Some of the activities use similar starting points to those provided in previous years, but with the aim of taking the learning further and deeper.

Based on the subject content for Key Stage 2 (outlined on the previous page), progression in Year 6 can be summarised as follows:

Performing in solo and ensemble contexts

As with previous years, children are given various opportunities to perform both vocal and instrumental music. They continue to practise singing in two-part harmony, and refine their singing skills by improving their diction, expression and articulation. Children continue to play more complex pieces that include a number of different layers. They learn to perform more complicated rhythms, and practise playing melodies with fluency and accuracy.

Improvising and composing music

During Year 6 children should continue to show a greater control and sophistication in selecting and combining sounds and musical phrases. They develop their ability to compose effective melodies, and add harmony to some of their pieces. They learn how to structure compositions into contrasting sections, and pay more attention to using the different dimensions effectively as they compose.

Listening with attention to detail

In Year 6 children continue to listen to recorded extracts of music and analyse them through verbal responses. Children should continue to build up their technical vocabulary in order to describe the music they hear. They also continue to listen to and evaluate their own compositions. They should find it easier to describe which bits of a composition are most successful, or which need more work, and why.

Using staff and other notations

Children continue to develop their ability to perform from and compose with various types of notation, including one-line staves and staff notation. They use number lines to notate more complex rhythms, and learn about some of the methods that composers have used to notate extended techniques.

Appreciating and understanding a wide range of music

Through the listening and performing activities in Year 6, children should continue to increase their understanding of different types of music, including the characteristics that identify different genres or styles.

Developing an understanding of the history of music

Children continue to develop a familiarity with the history of music. They consolidate their understanding of how music has changed over time, and recognise some of the musical differences between pieces from contrasting periods.

Medium-term planning Autumn 1

W	Activity summary	Curriculum objectives	Outcomes
1	Children develop rhythmic ostinatos using number lines (for example, numbers 1 to 8 in a row where certain numbers are circled to indicate the beats that children should play). Some of the ostinatos can be regular (for example, numbers 1 and 5 are circled) and others irregular (for example, numbers 2, 6 and 8 are circled). Children explore different timbres for the ostinatos. In groups they layer their ostinatos and practise playing them simultaneously.	• Understand and explore how music is created using appropriate musical notations. • Perform music.	• Can maintain a complex rhythmic ostinato against a number of contrasting parts.
2	Children continue their work from the previous week. They practise playing their ostinatos in groups, maintaining rhythmic accuracy and increasing the tempo where possible. Encourage children to swap parts so everyone gets a chance to play regular and irregular ostinatos.	• Understand and explore how music is created using appropriate musical notations. • Perform music.	• Can maintain a complex rhythmic ostinato against a number of contrasting parts.
3	Children review selected songs from the previous year (including at least one song in two-part harmony). Encourage children to sing with a greater accuracy in pitch and rhythm. Vocal warm-ups can help with this. Children should also aim to sing more expressively, paying attention to their dynamics and articulation.	• Learn to sing and to use their voices.	• Can recall songs learned during the previous year. • Can sing with greater accuracy in pitch and rhythm.
4	Children watch a selection of TV adverts with contrasting music. They discuss how the music is effective in helping to advertise the products. Give children a selection of three or four contrasting music extracts and three or four products. Children have to decide which music they would use to advertise which products, explaining their reasoning with musical vocabulary.	• Listen to, review and evaluate music.	• Can describe an extract of music using appropriate language. • Can think about the message or effect of an extract of music.
5	Children learn a new two-part song. They continue to develop their ability to maintain a vocal part against a contrasting one.	• Learn to sing and to use their voices.	• Can maintain a vocal part against a contrasting one.
6	Review any work from the half term that might require further consolidation. Consider combining some or all of the activities that have been covered during this half term into a whole-class performance or presentation.		

Medium-term planning Autumn 2

W	Activity summary	Curriculum objectives	Outcomes
1	Children compose melodies and notate them using one-line staves or staff notation. They aim to use some of the composition techniques mentioned in Year 5, Autumn 2, Week 1. Children then add accompaniments to their melodies. These could consist of drones, chords, bass lines or rhythmic ostinatos. Children could also explore using music technology to add chords or atmospheric sound effects.	• Create and compose music. • Understand and explore how music is created using appropriate musical notations. • Use technology appropriately.	• Can compose a melody and accompaniment. • Can notate a melody using one-line staves or staff notation.
2	Children continue their work from the previous week. They refine, perform and evaluate their pieces.	• Create and compose music. • Perform music.	• Can perform a melody with an accompaniment.
3	Children listen to a piece of music written before the 20th century and a contrasting, contemporary cover version of the same piece (for example, the opening of Beethoven's Fifth Symphony and Walter Murphy's 'A Fifth of Beethoven'). They discuss and list the similarities and differences between the two pieces.	• Listen to, review and evaluate music.	• Can compare and contrast two pieces of music.
4	Similar to Year 5, Spring 1, Week 4, children compose a short song. They could use a poem they have written in one of their English lessons for the lyrics. Children should focus on creating a catchy melody that is fun to sing. They could also add a simple accompaniment, such as a rhythmic ostinato or some basic chords.	• Create and compose music.	• Can compose a song.
5	Children continue their work from the previous week. They rehearse and perform their songs. The whole class then tries to learn one or more of the songs. Children take an active role in teaching their songs to each other.	• Create and compose music. • Perform music.	• Can perform a song as part of a small group. • Can take part in peer learning.
6	Review any work from the half term that might require further consolidation. Consider combining some or all of the activities that have been covered during this half term into a whole-class performance or presentation.		

Medium-term planning Spring 1

W	Activity summary	Curriculum objectives	Outcomes
1	Similar to Year 6, Autumn 1, Week 1, children use number lines to create regular and irregular rhythmic ostinatos. In groups they layer up the ostinatos and practise performing them simultaneously. Children can increase the complexity of the ostinatos by introducing different dimensions such as pitch, dynamics or timbre (for example, an ostinato could include high and low notes or loud and quiet notes).	• Create and compose music. • Perform music.	• Can maintain a complex rhythmic ostinato against a number of contrasting parts.
2	Children consolidate their work on rhythmic ostinatos by learning a traditional piece of African drumming (which could be played on any classroom percussion instruments). This piece could include sections of call and response and opportunities for the children to improvise. As part of this week's work, children could learn about African culture and music.	• Perform music.	• Can maintain a complex ostinato against a number of contrasting parts.
3	Children refine their singing skills by concentrating on their phrasing and diction. They practise singing tongue twisters and then see how long they can hold a note using one breath. Children revise a song they know well, concentrating on their diction and phrasing (for example, breathing together in appropriate places, and holding notes at the end of a phrase for the correct length of time).	• Learn to sing and to use their voices.	• Can sing with attention to diction and phrasing.
4	In groups, children create an arrangement of a pop tune or melody that they know well. They can try varying the tune itself as well as creating an accompaniment for it. To make this activity more challenging, children could be given the task of changing the mood of the tune (for example, making a fast, upbeat tune sound slow and sad). Children could use classroom instruments or music technology to create an arrangement (or a combination of both).	• Create and compose music. • Use technology appropriately.	• Can create an arrangement of a melody.
5	Children continue their work from the previous week. They refine, perform and evaluate their arrangements. If children have been tasked with giving their arrangements a contrasting mood, they could evaluate how successful they were at this. *Is the mood of the arrangement noticeably different to that of the original? If not, how could the contrast be improved?*	• Create and compose music. • Perform music. • Listen to, review and evaluate music.	• Can create and perform an arrangement of a melody.
6	Review any work from the half term that might require further consolidation. Consider combining some or all of the activities that have been covered during this half term into a whole-class performance or presentation.		

Notes:
Visit the Scholastic website (www.scholastic.co.uk/100music) to find a sample lesson covering week 1's work on using number lines to create regular and irregular rhythmic ostinatos.

YEAR 6

Medium-term planning Spring 2

YEAR 6

W	Activity summary	Curriculum objectives	Outcomes
1	In pairs, one child plays a melody and another accompanies it with a bass line. Children then swap roles. They practise playing in time together and listening to each other. This week's work could be used as an opportunity to practise reading from notation.	• Perform music.	• Can perform a melody or bass line as part of a duo.
2	In pairs, children compose a new bass line to accompany the melody from the previous week. They practise playing both parts together. If there is time, children could listen to and evaluate each other's bass lines. This activity can be used to explore the concept of harmony. *Which bass lines sound the most pleasing against the melody and which sound like they clash with it? Why is this?*	• Create and compose music. • Perform music.	• Can compose a bass line to accompany a melody. • Can perform a melody or bass line as part of a duo.
3	Improvise short phrases and sing them to the class. Children have to repeat each phrase in a call-and-response manner. Children then form a circle. All children sing a short phrase ('the call'). One child is selected to improvise an answering phrase ('the response'). All children repeat this phrase (so it becomes the next call). Another child improvises an answer (the response), and so on.	• Learn to sing and to use their voices.	• Can repeat short musical phrases by ear. • Can improvise calls and responses.
4	Similar to Year 4, Summer, 1 Week 1, children learn an ensemble piece (where there are a number of different layers to the piece, played on different instruments). Children learn their parts by reading them from staff notation (with help, where necessary). Encourage children to use any instruments they have been learning as an extra-curricular activity.	• Understand and explore how music is created using appropriate musical notations. • Have the opportunity to learn a musical instrument.	• Can perform in an ensemble piece. • Can read simple staff notation.
5	Children continue to rehearse the piece from the previous week. They aim for greater accuracy, control and expression in their playing.	• Understand and explore how music is created using appropriate musical notations. • Have the opportunity to learn a musical instrument.	• Can perform in an ensemble piece. • Can read simple staff notation.
6	Review any work from the half term that might require further consolidation. Consider combining some or all of the activities that have been covered during this half term into a whole-class performance or presentation.		

■SCHOLASTIC

Medium-term planning Summer 1

W	Activity summary	Curriculum objectives	Outcomes
1	Similar to Year 5, Summer 1, Week 1, children use the rhythms of a rhyme or chant as a stimulus for creating melodic ostinatos based on a pentatonic scale. Children practise playing their ostinatos fluently. Once they are confident with this, they can compose small variations and add them into repetitions of the ostinato. Children could also add drones or simple chords to their ostinatos as an accompaniment.	• Create and compose music. • Have the opportunity to learn a musical instrument.	• Can compose melodic ostinatos using a pentatonic scale. • Can perform melodic ostinatos fluently.
2	Children continue their work from the previous week. In groups, they combine their ostinatos to create longer compositions. They rehearse and perform their pieces to the rest of the class.	• Perform music.	• Can perform melodic ostinatos fluently.
3	Children are presented with a few different programme notes (brief descriptions about a piece of music). They have to match up the programme notes to the correct extracts of music. As they listen to the music, they discuss and evaluate which notes most closely correspond to each extract. Children then identify the main instruments playing in each extract, matching them up to a selection of pictures.	• Listen to, review and evaluate music.	• Can identify a piece of music from a written description. • Can identify instruments by ear and name them correctly.
4	As a whole class, children add an accompaniment to a song they know well. The accompaniment could potentially include various rhythmic ostinatos, a bass line and some simple chords. Children practise performing the song and accompaniment together (some children could just sing or play, while others might be able to do both).	• Learn to sing and to use their voices.	• Can perform a song and its accompaniment as a group.
5	Children continue their work from the previous week. They rehearse and perform the song, using a recording device to capture their performance. Encourage children to swap parts during the course of the lesson so everyone is given a chance to play the accompaniment and sing the melody.	• Learn to sing and to use their voices. • Use technology appropriately.	• Can perform a song and its accompaniment as a group. • Can use technology to record a performance.
6	Review any work from the half term that might require further consolidation. Consider combining some or all of the activities that have been covered during this half term into a whole-class performance or presentation.		

Medium-term planning Summer 2

W	Activity summary	Curriculum objectives	Outcomes
1	Children explore extended techniques: unusual ways of singing or playing instruments. They see how many different sounds they can create from their own voices and instruments. Children devise symbols to notate the most interesting sounds. This activity could be used to explore 20th century music and graphic notation (such as the works of John Cage and Luciano Berio).	• Have the opportunity to learn a musical instrument. • Understand and explore how music is created using appropriate musical notations.	• Can use extended techniques on a variety of instruments. • Can invent appropriate symbols to represent different sounds.
2	Children continue their work from the previous week. In groups, they compose short pieces using extended techniques, and notate the results using their own notation.	• Create and compose music. • Understand and explore how music is created using appropriate musical notations.	• Can compose and notate a piece using extended techniques.
3	Children learn about different ways to structure a composition (for example, using binary, ternary and rondo forms). In groups, they use one of these structures to compose a piece with at least two contrasting sections. The piece should involve more than one layer (for example, a melody and accompaniment).	• Create and compose music.	• Can compose a piece with contrasting sections.
4	Children continue their work from the previous week. They refine, rehearse and perform their compositions.	• Create and compose music. • Perform music.	• Can compose and perform a piece with contrasting sections.
5 & 6	Review any work from the half term that might require further consolidation. Children rehearse performances of some of the songs, pieces or compositions that have been learned or created during the year. These are presented in an end-of-year showcase or concert.	• Perform music.	• Can rehearse and perform music to a high standard.

Notes:
Visit the Scholastic website (www.scholastic.co.uk/100music) to find a sample lesson covering week 3's work on learning about different ways to structure a composition.

Year 6 Background knowledge

Using number lines

Various activities in this year make use of 'number lines', which can be effective in challenging children to get to grips with more complex rhythms (and to count carefully!). A number line is simply a series of numbers where certain numbers are circled, for example:

①　2　3　4　⑤　6　7　8

Children count to eight and clap or play a sound on the circled numbers. They keep repeating the rhythm in a loop.

More complex rhythms can be layered on top of this. For example, while a child loops the number line above, another could loop the one below at the same time:

1　②　3　4　5　⑥　7　⑧

Working with bass lines and harmony

As children progress with their composition work they will start to use simple chords and bass lines to accompany their melodies. At Key Stage 2, children are not expected to have enough theoretical knowledge to make informed choices about suitable chords and harmonies. Harmonising a melody will therefore have to be done by ear, using a trial-and-error approach. However, children should begin to sense whether a bass note or chord sounds pleasing against a given note in the melody, or whether it seems to clash with the melody.

Using extended techniques

The activity in Summer 2, Week 1 makes use of extended techniques: unconventional methods of singing or playing instruments. Examples include playing a guitar with a violin bow, beatboxing into a flute or singing in an unusual voice (such as a growl or whisper). Many 20th-century composers have used extended techniques and found inventive ways to notate them; if children wish to study their music as a model for their own, good places to start are with John Cage's works for prepared piano or Luciano Berio's *Sequenzas*.

Structuring compositions

The activity in Summer 2, Week 3 requires children to compose to a specific structure. Three of the simplest structures that composers often use are binary, ternary and rondo forms. The simplest way to describe these structures is with different letters:

- Binary = AB
- Ternary = ABA
- Rondo = ABACA.

Each letter represents a contrasting section. For example, in rondo form a tune is heard three times (A) with two contrasting tunes in-between each repeat (B and C).

Progression across the key stages

In order to plan effectively for progression in music education, it is necessary to have some understanding of how children develop musically during Key Stages 1 and 2. One problem to be aware of is that musical development is rarely linear or uniform; children can present very different capabilities and understanding at the same age. There are a variety of reasons for this, the most common being that children dedicate very different amounts of time to making music outside of school.

Steady development can be encouraged by providing regular and frequent opportunities for musical learning. So rather than simply timetabling in a single music lesson per week, look for opportunities for children to engage in musical activity at other times. Encourage making use of breaks, lunchtimes and after-school clubs. In addition, try to find ways of making connections between musical activity at home and school. Revisiting musical learning is essential to ensure steady musical progression.

Many of the activities presented in this book have a single main focus, but always try to integrate listening, composing and performing activities as much as possible. Finally, remember that progress depends on finding and striking the right balance between the security of building on your children's current musical understanding and competencies, and the challenges presented by stretching and broadening their musical horizons.

Progression in singing

Key Stage 1

Year 1	Year 2
Sing expressively and creatively through learning a simple repertoire of songs. (NC)	Sing expressively and creatively through learning a simple repertoire of songs. (NC) Gain confidence in singing in smaller groups or as a soloist.

Key Stage 2

Year 3	Year 4	Year 5	Year 6
Sing with increasing accuracy, fluency, control and expression. (NC) Learn a wider, more complex range of songs.	Sing with increasing accuracy, fluency, control and expression. (NC) Learn a wider, more complex range of songs. Sing in two-part harmony.	Sing with increasing accuracy, fluency, control and expression. (NC) Learn a wider, more complex range of songs. Sing in two-part harmony. Compose and perform a song.	Sing with increasing accuracy, fluency, control and expression. (NC) Learn a wider, more complex range of songs. Sing in two-part harmony. Compose and perform a song.

Progression in listening and appraising

Key Stage 1

Year 1	Year 2
Listen with concentration and understanding to a range of high-quality live and recorded music. (NC)	Listen with concentration and understanding to a range of high-quality live and recorded music. (NC) Learn to listen critically to a composition in order to identify its strengths and weaknesses.

Key Stage 2

Year 3	Year 4	Year 5	Year 6
Listen with attention to detail and recall sounds with increasing aural memory. (NC) Appreciate and understand a wide range of high-quality live and recorded music drawn from different traditions. (NC) Describe music using appropriate musical vocabulary.	Listen with attention to detail and recall sounds with increasing aural memory. (NC) Appreciate and understand a wide range of high-quality live and recorded music drawn from different traditions. (NC) Describe music using appropriate musical vocabulary.	Listen with attention to detail and recall sounds with increasing aural memory. (NC) Appreciate and understand a wide range of high-quality live and recorded music drawn from different traditions. (NC) Describe music using appropriate musical vocabulary.	Listen with attention to detail and recall sounds with increasing aural memory. (NC) Appreciate and understand a wide range of high-quality live and recorded music drawn from different traditions. (NC) Describe music using appropriate musical vocabulary.

Progression in composing

Key Stage 1

Year 1	Year 2
Experiment with, create, select and combine sounds using the inter-related dimensions of music. (NC)	Experiment with, create, select and combine sounds using the inter-related dimensions of music. (NC) Begin to think more carefully about the structure of a composition.

Key Stage 2

Year 3	Year 4	Year 5	Year 6
Improvise and compose music for a range of purposes using the inter-related dimensions of music. (NC) Use and understand staff and other musical notations. (NC) Create compositions with more than one layer.	Improvise and compose music for a range of purposes using the inter-related dimensions of music. (NC) Use and understand staff and other musical notations. (NC) Create compositions with a number of layers.	Improvise and compose music for a range of purposes using the inter-related dimensions of music. (NC) Use and understand staff and other musical notations. (NC) Create compositions with a number of layers. Compose effective melodies.	Improvise and compose music for a range of purposes using the inter-related dimensions of music. (NC) Use and understand staff and other musical notations. (NC) Create compositions with a number of layers. Compose effective melodies.

Progression in playing musical instruments

Key Stage 1

Year 1	Year 2
Play tuned and untuned instruments musically. (NC) Perform simple melodies and rhythm patterns.	Play tuned and untuned instruments musically. (NC) Gain a greater control over pitch and rhythm.

Key Stage 2

Year 3	Year 4	Year 5	Year 6
Play with increasing accuracy, fluency, control and expression. (NC) Play and perform in solo and ensemble contexts. (NC)	Play with increasing accuracy, fluency, control and expression. (NC) Play and perform in solo and ensemble contexts. (NC) Play increasingly complex pieces that require control over both pitch and rhythm.	Play with increasing accuracy, fluency, control and expression. (NC) Play and perform in solo and ensemble contexts. (NC) Play increasingly complex pieces that require control over both pitch and rhythm.	Play with increasing accuracy, fluency, control and expression. (NC) Play and perform in solo and ensemble contexts. (NC) Play increasingly complex pieces that require control over both pitch and rhythm.

Glossary of musical terms

Term	Definition
Articulation	Altering the way notes sound by using different playing techniques
Beat	The repeating steady beat, underpinning a piece of music
Body percussion	Striking the body in various ways to make percussive sounds
Call and response	A pair of musical phrases which complement one another
Drone	A continuous note or chord
Duration	How long or short notes are
Dynamics	Refers to the softness or loudness of a piece of music
Elements (i.e. musical elements/dimensions)	The distinguishing features of music: pitch, rhythm, duration, dynamics, timbre and structure
Graphic notation	The use of visual symbols to represent music
Improvise	Creating music on the spot
Motif	A short musical idea
MP3 recorder	An audio recording machine – saves the recordings as mp3 files
One-line stave	A single line which can be used to represent high/middle/low notes
Ostinato	A musical phrase which repeats
Pitch	A measure of the frequency or how high or low notes are
Programmatic music	Music which attempts to tell a story through sound
Pulse	The repeating steady beat, underpinning a piece of music
Rhythm	Patterns created by notes of various lengths
Rhythm grid	A table which can be used to indicate where notes are played in a rhythm pattern
Sample	A short recorded sound
Soundscape	A collage of sounds that conveys a mood or environment
Staff notation	The standard five-line musical notation system
Tempo	The speed of a piece of music
Texture	The number of layers in a piece of music
Timbre	The tonal quality or sound of an instrument that distinguishes it from others
Warm ups	Routines that prepare players for musical activity

Fully in line with the new curriculum objectives

SCHOLASTIC

Essential support for the 2014 National Curriculum

Plan with confidence with 100 Lessons Planning Guides
Complete planning frameworks with long and medium-term guidance for Years 1-6

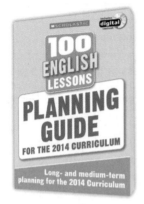
9781407128399

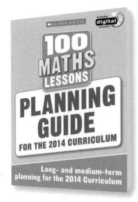
9781407128405

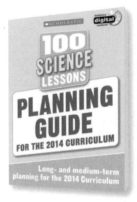
9781407128412

9781407128610

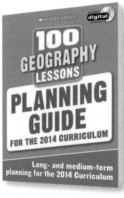
9781407128597

9781407128603

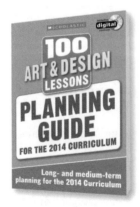
9781407140865

9781407140858

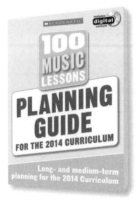
9781407140841

Order at www.scholastic.co.uk/100lessons or call us on 0845 603 9091